U0558871

The Macat Library
世界思想宝库钥匙丛书

解析菲利普·津巴多

《路西法效应》

AN ANALYSIS OF

PHILIP ZIMBARDO'S

THE LUCIFER EFFECT

Alexander J. O'Connor ◎ 著

单文波 ◎ 译

上海外语教育出版社
SHANGHAI FOREIGN LANGUAGE EDUCATION PRESS

目　录

CONTENTS

引言

要 点

- 菲利普·津巴多，生于 1933 年，美国社会心理学家、斯坦福大学荣退教授。社会心理学 * 研究社会环境如何影响人们的思维过程、记忆、学习和行为。津巴多因其在特定环境对行为的影响方面开展的突破性研究而闻名。

- 在 2007 年出版的《路西法效应》中，津巴多详细地描述了产生邪恶的情境力量 *（分析重点是外部环境的某些方面）。此处的邪恶是指故意给他人造成生理、心理、经济或情感方面的伤害以及痛苦的人和行为。

- 津巴多以独到的眼光在书中详尽分析了情境如何以及为什么会使人们产生从众 * 心理，去认同一个邪恶的想法。当个体由于强大的社会压力而不得不强迫自己顺应群体的思维过程和行为方式时，从众行为就产生了。

菲利普·津巴多其人

菲利普·津巴多，《路西法效应：好人是如何变成恶魔的》一书的作者，出生于纽约市布朗克斯南部，津巴多后来称该地区是一个贫民区 *（即贫民窟，其居民通常来自一个单一少数族裔）。他童年的大部分时间正赶上那场从 1929 年一直持续到 1930 年代末的经济大萧条 *，那是一场严重的经济衰退，给大部分美国人造成了极大的经济困难。津巴多自己也是在贫穷中长大。

在 2007 年出版的《路西法效应》中，津巴多描述了环境如何影响他的思维方式和后来的职业生涯。他写道："发展有用的'街头智慧'是都市贫民区的生存法则。你得要知道谁会算计你，谁能帮你，要躲着谁，要讨好谁。"[1] 津巴多解释说，这些经历让自己明白了权力和特定情境在影响行为和生活结果方面扮演的关键角色。

他的成长经历促使他对心理学产生了兴趣。1959 年，津巴多在耶鲁大学获得心理学博士学位。自 1968 年起，他一直在加利福尼亚州的斯坦福大学心理学系执教。现在津巴多虽为该大学的荣退教授，但他仍旧活跃于研究工作和政治活动中。

2012 年，他写道，自从 1971 年主持了"斯坦福监狱实验"*这项重要研究以后，他就"成为一个呼吁监狱改革的积极分子。"[2] 他经常给政策制定者们和司法部门提出建议，并向他们说明监狱对囚犯的负面心理影响。他还创立了"致力于激发每日英雄行为"的研究机构——"英雄创想计划"*。

除了经济大萧条之外，还有两个重大的社会政治事件影响了津巴多和他的研究。一个是 20 世纪 50 年代，许多社会心理学家开始研究权力、服从和邪恶等话题，意图解释在第二次世界大战*（1939—1945）期间发生的一系列骇人听闻的事件和残暴行为。这场全球性的大战始于德国入侵波兰，并最终使众多国家卷入其中。这也引发了津巴多的研究兴趣。另外一个是，他反对美国军事介入越南战争*（1955—1975），即北越和南越（1961 年后得到美国支持）之间的武装冲突，他的立场也促使他积极投身到政治和社会活动中。

《路西法效应》的主要内容

《路西法效应》旨在从心理学层面解释邪恶是怎么产生的。

虽然津巴多没有在书中明确给邪恶下定义，但他依据历史上发生的"暴力、匿名、侵略、破坏、摧残和恐怖"[3] 等具体事件为其认为的邪恶提供了一个隐含的框架。他特别关注在 2003 年美国领导的多国联军入侵伊拉克期间，一些美国军人在伊拉克阿布格莱布监狱＊犯下的虐囚罪行。

在这个案例中，负责在阿布格莱布监狱看押伊拉克战俘的美军人员对这些囚犯进行了多次严重的生理、心理和性侵害，并经常拍照记录下这些行为。对许多目击者而言，这是一起令人震惊的施虐＊行为实例（施虐狂指从暴力、残忍或给他人造成痛苦中取乐的人）。但津巴多认为，发生在阿布格莱布监狱的虐囚事件并不令人意外，因为他在 1971 年主持的斯坦福监狱实验揭示了任何普通人——甚至有些坚信自己绝不会伤害他人——都有能力干出被津巴多称为"邪恶"的勾当。

在《路西法效应》一书中，津巴多传递了一条核心信息，那就是情境对我们影响巨大。为了说明这一点，他详细描述并分析了自己在斯坦福大学亲自设计和开展的斯坦福监狱实验。一共 24 名志愿者参与其中，他们同意在一个临时的监狱中生活或工作两个星期。津巴多和他的研究助手随机给他们分配角色，要么当囚犯，要么当狱卒，而他本人则担任典狱长。狱卒们接到指令，必须维持监狱秩序，于是他们很快就开始滥用自己的权力。津巴多发现，狱卒们从心理和生理上折磨囚犯。仅仅过了 6 天，实验就被紧急叫停。

津巴多在 26 年后出版的《路西法效应》一书中指出，当时受到整个局面和众多情境因素的影响，狱卒的心态发生了重大变化。他指出，斯坦福监狱实验"有力地证明了不良的制度和情境隐藏着巨大的危害，会让好人做出与其本性相异的病态行为。"[4]

在书中，津巴多利用他从斯坦福监狱实验中获得的详细调查结果，以及此后开展的辅助性研究，分析了历史上其他一些令人发指、手段残酷的罪恶行径，尤其关注了阿布格莱布监狱的虐囚事件。

就像斯坦福监狱实验一样，津巴多本人也参与了阿布格莱布监狱虐囚事件的调查。在对其中一个狱卒伊万·弗里德里克*的审讯中，津巴多担任了专家证人，伊万最后因在狱中袭击和虐待囚犯而被定罪。社会心理学家罗伯特·莱文*在评论《路西法效应》时写道："津巴多讲述了弗里德里克如何从一个充满理想主义的士兵彻底变成一个残忍的施暴者，故事临近结尾之时，人们感觉阿布格莱布监狱面目狰狞，和斯坦福监狱实验场景毫无二致，好像是人格扭曲的社会心理学家设计了这个伊拉克监狱，目的就是要复制津巴多的实验，只不过这次是真正的狱卒和犯人罢了。"5

最后，津巴多讨论了系统性因素*（诸如政府、文化、经济制度和组织机构这些庞大系统的影响）如何逐步设置恶劣的条件，滋生恶劣的情境，进而诱发罪恶行为。这本书的结尾研究了人们如何能避免恶劣的情境并抵抗强迫作恶的情境压力*，就像津巴多主张英雄行为也是在情境中产生的一样。这些情境压力是一种心理上的压力，无论人们是否意识到，周围环境都会将这种压力施加在他们身上。

《路西法效应》的学术价值

尽管《路西法效应》包含了诸多关于社会心理学、研究伦理方面的内容和大量历史事件，但是这本书之所以重要，主要是因为它对津巴多亲自主导的斯坦福监狱实验进行了深入的调查。这项实验在当今被公认为心理学领域的一项重大研究。在审视这项实验时，津巴多描述了他认为造成斯坦福监狱实验结果的主要社会和心理因素（也解释了造成阿布格莱布监狱虐囚等罪行的原因）。他还分析了安然造假丑闻＊（2001 年发生在美国能源公司安然公司的一起大范围公司腐败和财务造假案件）、卢旺达种族大屠杀＊（占卢旺达人口多数的胡图族于 1994 年发动了一场大屠杀，多达一百万人被害，其中绝大多数是占人口少数的图西族）以及罗马天主教会性侵丑闻＊（最近几十年在全世界范围内发生的多起天主教神职人员性侵事件）。

然而，津巴多让《路西法效应》的读者看到了希望，他还给他们提出建议，以使他们能够更好地理解这些"邪恶"行为："我曾经提议，当我们尝试解释变态的行为和表面上的人格变化时，应该比以往更多地考虑和重视情境和系统过程，因为人类行为总是受制于情境压力。"6

最重要的是，津巴多希望，如果人们多了解这些危险的情境力量，就能够在生活中察觉和抵抗在特定环境中逼迫他们做坏事的强大压力："在引用的研究和真实案例中，总会有一些人能够抵制（情境影响和罪恶），不屈从于诱惑。能够远离邪恶并不是因为他们天生就有上苍赐予的美丽心灵，而更可能是直觉上深知心理和社会的抵抗策略。"7

在津巴多看来，英雄行为就像邪恶一样，也并非与生俱来，而是任何人，包括他的读者，都可以学习培养的。

最后，在《路西法效应》一书中，津巴多对斯坦福监狱实验引发的一些争议提出了深刻的见解并梳理了一些更为宽泛的概念。实际上，津巴多在整本书中都提及了这些争议，其中主要一项就是有人批评这项实验有违道德。就此，他也提出了自己的分析和历史背景。同时，津巴多专辟一章探讨研究伦理和斯坦福监狱实验，和大家讨论他对这项实验伦理的看法和他在遵守伦理方面的失误。

1. 菲利普·津巴多:《路西法效应:好人是如何变成恶魔的》,纽约:兰登书屋,2007年,第 xi 页。

2. 斯考特·德鲁里、斯考特·A. 赫琴斯、杜安·E. 夏特沃斯和卡罗尔·L. 怀特:"菲利普·G. 津巴多谈职业生涯和斯坦福监狱实验 40 周年纪念",《心理学历史》第 15 卷,2012 年第 2 期,第 162 页。

3. 津巴多:《路西法效应》,第 xi 页。

4. 津巴多:《路西法效应》,第 195 页。

5. 罗伯特·莱文:"人犯下的罪行",《美国科学家》,2007 年 9—10 月,登录日期 2015 年 9 月 15 日,http://americanscientist.org/bookshelf/content2/2007/5/the-evil-that-men-do。

6. 津巴多:《路西法效应》,第 445 页。

7. 津巴多:《路西法效应》,第 xiii 页。

第一部分：学术渊源

1 作者生平与历史背景

要点 🗝

- 《路西法效应》极为详尽地分析了津巴多在 1971 年开展的著名的斯坦福监狱实验 *。津巴多借助实验的研究结论，对最近发生的真实罪恶行径提出了深刻见解，这让该实验又有了新的意义。

- 津巴多学生时代就在纽约剧院区打工。他逐渐懂得如何欣赏戏剧、如何提高制作水准（有助于提升剧场体验的细节和技巧），这一点在他后来设计的斯坦福监狱实验中体现得淋漓尽致。

- 几次重大历史事件，特别是美国 1929 年经济大滑坡造成的大萧条和美国在 1961—1975 年间卷入的伤亡巨大的越南战争，促使津巴多从事社会心理学研究（研究社会环境如何影响人们的思想和行为），并且积极投身于政治和社会活动。

为何要读这部著作？

菲利普·津巴多撰写的《路西法效应：好人是如何变成恶魔的》（2007）描述了一些会导致普通人做出违反道德、变态、具有毁灭性和"邪恶"行为的情境 * 因素（如背景、环境等影响研究对象的外在因素）。政治学家罗丝·麦克德莫特 * 在评论《路西法效应》时写道："所有对心理过程和政治现实交叉领域感兴趣的人，都有必要读一读这部新书，这本书由经典的斯坦福监狱实验设计者撰写，引人入胜，极为出色。"[1]

《路西法效应》中大多数经验性数据（可通过观察验证的数据）是津巴多从他著名的 1971 年斯坦福监狱实验记录中提取的。这项研究表明，普通人如果置身于某些特定环境中，很快就可以变得"邪恶"。这项研究至今仍然称得上是社会心理学领域中最著名、最具戏剧性、最重要的一项实验。正如社会心理学家罗伯特·莱文描述的那样："斯坦福监狱实验已经成为社会心理学领域的一块奠基石……在斯坦福发生的一切清楚地表明疯狂的环境会导致疯狂的行为，甚至连正常人也不例外。"[2]

斯坦福监狱实验也成为心理学领域受到思考和分析最多的研究之一。然而，在《路西法效应》一书中，早已有重大影响的斯坦福监狱实验又被津巴多注入了新的生机。当津巴多在解释 20 世纪 70 年代以来全世界范围内的多项罪行时，他结合了对实验的原初和最新诠释，并介绍了近年来的研究成果。津巴多提供了迄今为止最全面的实验记录——包括对整个实验过程的生动重述、实验记录和对参与者的采访。

在书中，津巴多还介绍了他对斯坦福监狱实验的新认识。他解释说，他已逐渐将许多导致犯罪发生的情境视作由系统性因素（大规模组织和系统的影响）所导致。因此，他认为这些系统性因素是值得心理学家研究的。

> "我估计，你会说我一开始就是个直觉力很强的心理学家，也是个'情境决定论者'*。我出生在纽约市布朗克斯南部的一个贫民区，我是在家出生的，两只手先出来。当时正值大萧条，在我的童年时期，我们搬了 31 次家。"
>
> —— 菲利普·津巴多："心理学研究成果公益服务 50 年纪念：
> 菲利普·津巴多专访"

作者生平

津巴多于 1933 年出生在纽约市一个赤贫如洗的城市贫民窟，在经济大萧条期间长大，缺衣少食。童年时期，他患有呼吸疾病，忍受着漫长的住院治疗。被隔离治疗期间，他目睹了周围很多生病的孩子相继死去。他后来回忆，"在个性形成的童年时期极度孤立的经历，不仅让我将来想成为一名心理学家，也让我想要从事研究工作，用行动去改善人类生活。"[3]

童年生活在城市的贫民区，讨好那些街头帮派，这些经历对津巴多一生影响很大。他回忆，他和朋友"为了加入那些团伙，都必须经过入会仪式，一天之内必须完成一系列的冒险任务，每个新手都是如此。"[4]入会背后的心理学变成了他日后研究工作的主题，其中包括斯坦福监狱实验。津巴多想要考察普通人是否真的愿意仅仅为了获得入会许可而放弃自己的道德标准和正常行为。

十几岁的时候，津巴多在纽约百老汇区的一个剧院打工。他后来回忆，"这段经历教给我一种优良品质——什么事情都一定要做好，"[5]这在后来精心制作和上演的斯坦福监狱实验中体现得特别明显。

后来，津巴多在耶鲁大学学习，并于 1959 年获得心理学博士学位。自 1968 年起，他担任斯坦福大学心理学教授，现为斯坦福大学荣退教授，继续致力于新领域的研究，其中包括：害羞、英雄主义、恐怖主义和时间观念。他同时也创立了"致力于激发每日英雄行为"的研究机构——英雄创想计划。

创作背景

津巴多承认，在他的童年和早期职业生涯中发生的三件重大社会政治事件对他产生了影响：大萧条、第二次世界大战和越南战争。首先，和美国大萧条时期的其他许多孩子一样，他也在贫寒中长大。他后来回忆，由于家庭的经济困境，他被评头论足，甚至不当人看，为此他感到痛苦无比。在一次采访中，津巴多说，"个人尊严受到伤害，这触发了我的好奇心，我很想知道这一认识是如何形成的，态度如何影响人们的行为，以及人们如何对自己一无所知的事情产生如此强烈的感受。"[6]

　　美国在 20 世纪 60 年代和 70 年代对越南的军事介入也影响了津巴多。他认为这是他后来积极参与政治和社会活动的起因。作为一名杰出的反战活动家，他还要求对美国的监狱系统实施变革。在 2012 年的专访中，津巴多说，"我有太多话要说，我现在可以利用我的知名度来推动某些事业的发展，比如反战、积极倡导和平，现在呢，我正在努力造就每日英雄。"[7]

1. 罗斯·麦克德莫特："回顾：《路西法效应：好人是如何变成恶魔的》津巴多著"，《政治心理学》第 28 卷，2007 年第 5 期，第 644 页。

2. 罗伯特·莱文："人犯下的罪行"，《美国科学家》，2007 年 9—10 月，登录日期 2015 年 9 月 15 日，http://americanscientist.org/bookshelf/content2/2007/5/the-evil-that-men-do。

3. 克里斯蒂娜·马斯拉奇："边缘皇帝"，《今日心理学》，2000 年 9 月 1 日，登录日期 2015 年 9 月 15 日，https://psychologytoday.com/articles/200009/emperor-the-edge。

4. 菲利普·津巴多："社会心理学家职业生涯回顾：专访菲利普·津巴多博士"，《社会行为和人格杂志》第 14 卷，1999 年第 1 期，第 2 页。

5. 乔治·M.斯拉维奇："心理学研究成果公益服务五十年纪念：专访菲利普·津

巴多",《心理学教学》第 36 卷,2009 年第 4 期,第 280 页。

6. 马斯拉奇:"边缘皇帝",《今日心理学》。

7. 斯考特·德鲁里、斯考特·A. 赫琴斯、杜安·E. 夏特沃斯和卡罗尔·L. 怀特: "菲利普·G. 津巴多谈职业生涯和斯坦福监狱实验 40 周年纪念",《心理学历史》 第 15 卷,2012 年第 2 期,第 164 页。

2 学术背景

要点 🔑

· 20 世纪 60 年代和 70 年代，在社会心理学家（研究周围社会环境如何影响人们的心理过程和行为的科学家）和人格心理学家 *（研究人们心理过程和行为方面的个体差异的科学家）之间展开了一场旷日持久的争论。争论的焦点是：情境因素和人格因素，哪个对个人行为影响更大？

· 社会心理学家穆扎弗·谢里夫 * 和所罗门·阿希 * 为情境力量决定行为这一论点提供了一些最强有力的证据。

· 耶鲁大学心理学教授斯坦利·米尔格拉姆 * 提供了更加生动的证据，证明了情境力量的作用。他的研究对菲利普·津巴多产生了较大影响。

著作语境

尽管菲利普·津巴多的《路西法效应：好人是如何变成恶魔的》于 2007 年出版，但这本书主要是对 1971 年斯坦福监狱实验的重述。所以，这本书是跨越两个时代的产物。

20 世纪 70 年代早期，心理学界正处于一场认知革命 * 之中。这场革命兴起于 20 世纪 50 年代，影响了众多学术领域，如心理学、人类学和语言学等。

认知革命总体来说是对行为主义 * 的偏离，行为主义主要研究可观察的行为，相反，认知革命关注对人类认知 * 的研究，也就是研究人们的心理、思想、态度、动机、心智能力、记忆和价值观等内心世界要素的内在活动。

津巴多专门从事社会心理学（研究社会环境如何影响人们的认知和行为）研究。社会心理学和其相关领域人格心理学（研究人们思维过程和行为的个体差异）也在争论：影响行为的首要因素是什么？究竟是个体及其内在态度——心理学家称之为性情＊——决定了行为，还是情境力量超过了个人的人格力量？

哥伦比亚大学心理学教授沃尔特·米歇尔＊经常被认为是这场所谓的"人格—情境之争"＊的发起者。米歇尔认为这是一场关于一致性的争论，"这种一致性使同一个人对于表面上相似的情境（也就是说引发相同的特质＊）有所反应，最重要的是，这是一场关于以整体特质推断为基础进行预测是否有效的争论。"[1]人格心理学中，"特质"指性情，即某种程度上一致的行为或认知模式。米歇尔对这些特质能否可靠而有意义地预测行为提出了质疑。

米歇尔认为，考虑性情、环境和它们之间的相互作用非常重要，这种方法被称为"互动主义"＊。然而，其他心理学家只集中于其中一种因素的研究。那时候，津巴多将情境视为决定行为的最重要因素。

在《路西法效应》2007年面世之时，大多数心理学家早已认可，性情因素（内在的性格特点，如人格特质）、情境因素（周围环境施加在个体身上的有意识或无意识的心理压力）以及它们之间的交互作用都是预测和解释行为不可缺少的部分。积极心理学＊作为近年来的一项研究课题，也在当时得到关注。积极心理学的倡导者意图改变心理学家长期以来提出的问题，从关注消极的结果，如人们如何以及为何会抑郁，转而关注积极的结果，如人们如何以及为何会健康向上。

> "从 20 世纪 50 年代开始，社会心理学领域关注的重点开始转向研究社会情境可能会给人们的思维、感觉和行为带来的强大的、有时甚至是违反直觉的影响。"
>
> —— 小卢迪·T. 本杰明*和杰弗里·A. 辛普森*:《情境的力量》

学科概览

20 世纪 50 年代中期，一大批社会心理学家已经成功地证明了情境因素对人类行为的决定性力量。一个确凿的早期例子是社会心理学家穆扎弗·谢里夫和卡罗琳·谢里夫*于 1954 年开展的"强盗山洞"实验*。在美国俄克拉荷马州的一个夏令营中，两位科学家将 22 名小男孩随机分为两组，并将孩子们置于一系列可操纵的情境之中。结果，孩子们的态度和行为发生了变化。在一系列的竞争任务中，他们你争我夺，加重了敌意和成见。另一方面，两组孩子合作完成任务以后，敌意和成见便减少了。

大约在同一时期，社会心理学家所罗门·阿希进行了一系列关于从众行为（由于社会压力，个人的思想和行为不得不服从群体的思想和行为）的研究，突出表现了情境对行为的决定性作用，而且往往是以意想不到的方式。在最经典的一次实验中，他给被试展示了一条黑色的线段，然后让大家从一组长度不一的黑色线段中找出一条和原先那条黑色线段相同长度的线段。然而其中一位被试并不知道，其他被试都是假被试，其实都是"托儿"。阿希事先"贿赂"了其他被试，让他们故意做出错误的选择。

这项实验清楚地说明了情境的力量和多数派的力量。尽管哪两条线段长度相等一目了然，但是被试在公共场合往往会做出错误选择，服从群体中多数人给出的答案。阿希的报告提到："一旦自信心动摇，相当一部分的被试都会服从群体的意见。人们一般认为真理在大多数人手里，这让他们无法下定决心报告他们自己的观察结果。"[2] 谢里夫和阿希的研究都证明了情境压力（比如当组成小组以后，可能接下来就会有人随大流）会使人们做出意料之外的行为。

学术渊源

在开展斯坦福监狱实验以及分析邪恶和英雄行为时，津巴多紧随谢里夫和阿希的步伐，认为情境和群体压力会产生重大影响。然而，心理学家斯坦利·米尔格拉姆——津巴多的朋友，也是他中学时期的同班同学——对他产生了最为直接的影响。津巴多后来回忆，早在中学时期，米尔格拉姆就对情境的力量很着迷："米尔格拉姆甚至在那个时候就关注大屠杀……他之所以进行盲从权威的研究，是因为他担心同样的事情会不会在这儿（美国）发生。"[3] "大屠杀"指的是纳粹德国及其元首阿道夫·希特勒精心策划的种族灭绝计划。第二次世界大战期间，大约 600 万欧洲犹太人和其他少数族裔以及社会少数群体被害。

在 20 世纪 60 年代初，时任耶鲁大学心理学教授的米尔格拉姆进行了一项具有开创性的"服从权威"*实验。他吩咐志愿者对一个陌生人实施电击，他们被告知这是一个关于学习行为的实验。他们压根就不知道，事实上根本没有电击产生。尽管大多数参与者在实验中表现出害怕和痛苦的神情，但只是因为实验者要求他们不能停止，所以他们执行越来越强烈的电击；电击看起来令人痛苦，充满危险，可是最后许多人仍然将电击强度提升到了足以致命的程度。

米尔格拉姆的同事以及公众对这项颇具争议的实验的结果感到惊讶不已，这项研究在当时生动地展现了情境力量（以及人们天生对权威的服从）对行为的影响。津巴多后来表示，"（米尔格拉姆）率先提出了一个观点：你仅仅是认为或者声称自己不会去做某事，这是不够的。事实上，甚至假想你处于某一情境中也是不够的，因为真实的情境是具有强大改造作用的社会环境。"[4]

1. 沃尔特·米歇尔："走向认知的社会学习人格重塑"，《心理学评论》第 80 卷，1973 年第 4 期，第 255 页。

2. 所罗门·E. 阿希："独立与从众研究：I. 一致的少数派和一致的多数派的斗争"，《心理学专题：一般和应用》第 70 卷，1956 年第 9 期，第 70 页。

3. 乔治·M. 斯拉维奇："心理学研究成果公益服务五十年纪念：专访菲利普·津巴多"，《心理学教学》第 36 卷，2009 年第 4 期，第 279 页。

4. 斯拉维奇："心理学研究成果公益服务五十年纪念"，第 279 页。

3 主导命题

要 点 ✎┉

- 2003 年美国入侵伊拉克期间，在巴格达阿布格莱布监狱执行看守任务的美军人员对伊拉克战俘实施了身体虐待、性侵犯和酷刑折磨。同时，有人声称美国的心理学家也参与了这起虐囚事件。

- 许多社会心理学家和独立调查者认为阿布格莱布的虐囚事件在很大程度上要归咎于情境因素。

- 当阿布格莱布的一名监狱看守受审时，菲利普·津巴多以专家证人的身份出庭作证，引述了他的斯坦福监狱实验，并直言不讳地指出了情境因素在虐囚事件中可能扮演的角色。

核心问题

菲利普·津巴多的《路西法效应：好人是如何变成恶魔的》（2007）试图探讨并解释 2003 年发生在巴格达阿布格莱布监狱的虐囚事件。美军监狱看守在那里对伊拉克战俘实施了持续的心理和生理折磨以及性侵害，许多场景都有录像片段。

学界已经将津巴多视为研究服刑心态和施虐行为（以给别人造成痛苦为乐）的权威专家。他参与了 2004 年关于阿布格莱布监狱的辩论，并给《波士顿环球报》写了一篇评论说，"除非我们了解关于'为什么'的相互作用，否则我们永远不能够抵抗那种可以将普通人转变成作恶者的强大力量。"[1] 通过这种方式，津巴多敦促研究者和公众去思考阿布格莱布监狱案件中情境因素的重要性。

阿布格莱布监狱虐囚事件引起公众关注后不久，一些新闻报道声称美国心理学家也卷入了这场风波之中，他们使用各种手段折磨伊拉克战俘。很快另有报道暗指代表全美心理学家的科学和专业机构美国心理学会*也牵涉其中。这些报道声称美国心理学会过去一直在帮助美国政府寻找有效的审讯手段。人们开始质疑这些手段是否等同于酷刑，而该学会曾经明确禁止其成员支持使用酷刑。

2006 年，美国心理学会下属的道德和国家安全委员会重申了先前的立场，宣称"任何情况都不能成为使用酷刑的正当理由，包括执行法律、规定或命令。"[2] 然而，各种消息来源和报道继续指责该学会的成员和领导支持或使用了酷刑手段。凭借从斯坦福监狱实验获得的经验，津巴多以一种特殊的立场针对阿布格莱布监狱虐囚事件、美国政府动用酷刑以及心理学家在这两个争议事件中扮演的角色等问题发表了看法。

> "一张张照片令人毛骨悚然，记录着年轻的伊拉克战俘被美军士兵虐待的场面，诉说着人性的堕落。这次事件震惊了整个世界，迫使我们不得不承认一些深受我们爱戴的士兵竟然会犯下如此残暴、变态和丧尽天良的罪行。"
> —— 菲利普·津巴多："情境力量把好士兵变成了'坏苹果'"

参与者

大多数心理学家在谈及阿布格莱布监狱的虐囚事件以及军官和心理学家对酷刑采取容忍态度时，往往都会从情境角度进行解释。他们认为，犯罪者之所以犯罪，是因为受到了周围的大环境所造成的各种心理压力的影响。

为了证实这一论述，这些学者经常援引心理学家斯坦利·米尔格拉姆的服从权威研究（实验中志愿者根据权威人物的命令给陌生人实施电击）和菲利普·津巴多的斯坦福监狱实验（实验中普通人很快就开始虐待受他们控制的其他志愿者）。

社会心理学家苏珊·T. 菲斯克 * 在谈到阿布格莱布监狱虐囚事件时，称米尔格拉姆和津巴多的研究具有"启发意义"。她写道，"为了扮演强势的角色，一些士兵盲目从众，也像其他士兵一样虐待战俘，这种情况在斯坦福监狱实验中就已经体现出来。"[3] 菲斯克还提出，如果在制定官方政策时考虑到这些研究结果，将会大有裨益："就像军事法庭 * 认定犯罪一样，社会认为个人应对他们的行为负责。但是社会心理学家认为我们也应让操控社会环境的同事和上级负责。"[4]

2004 年，掌管军务的美国国防部 * 委托一个独立小组负责调查阿布格莱布监狱虐囚事件。该小组最终的调查结果也将罪责归咎于情境因素、监狱中的上级领导以及美国军方。同年，由詹姆斯·施莱辛格率领的一个委员会对阿布格莱布监狱的虐囚事件展开了一次独立调查，该委员会在施莱辛格报告 * 中提交了调查结果，并指出："虐囚事件发生的原因绝不只是个别士兵没有遵守制定的规范，也并不只是一些军官没有严格执行军事纪律。"[5] 委员会继续陈述说："存在着更高层面的制度和个人的责任。"[6]

当时的论战

津巴多通过学术途径和媒体渠道公开指出，阿布格莱布监狱中发生的虐囚事件和斯坦福监狱实验中的情形极为相似。根据斯坦福监狱实验的调查结果，津巴多认为情境和系统性因素是伊拉克监狱虐囚案件的最根本原因。2004 年，他给《波士顿环球报》写了一篇评论，谈到他认为卷入虐囚门的美军士兵可能"曾经是好苹果，但是放进了坏木桶，结果被腐化变质了。"[7]他还提及心理学家斯坦利·米尔格拉姆的服从权威研究来证实自己的观点。

不久之后，在 2004 年底，津巴多为美军前中士伊万·弗里德里克出庭辩护，后者因在阿布格莱布监狱虐待和折磨伊拉克囚犯而受到军事法庭审判（在军事法庭上被起诉）。作为辩护团队的代表，津巴多和其他心理学家以及医学专家评估了弗里德里克的心理健康史。津巴多后来在审判中担任专家证人。

津巴多在《路西法效应》中回忆了他的证词以及他如何"概述了……斯坦福监狱实验环境和阿布格莱布监狱虐囚环境之间的相似之处。"[8]他还"认为是情境导致了（弗里德里克）的变态行为，这名士兵为自己的行为深感懊悔和内疚。"[9]

社会心理学家和军方似乎都认为阿布格莱布监狱虐囚事件中存在明显的情境因素。然而，津巴多并不相信军事法庭收到了这份报告，他对弗里德里克受到的判决（包括在军事监狱中服刑 8 年）感到不满。津巴多认为，美国政府和军方真正希望采纳和宣扬的观点是："有少数的流氓士兵，是原本很好的美国军队这个大木桶里的'坏苹果'。"[10]

1. 菲利普·G. 津巴多："权力将好士兵变成'坏苹果'"，《波士顿环球报》，2004 年 9 月 5 日，登录日期 2015 年 9 月 16 日，http://www.boston.com/news/globe/editorial_opinion/oped/articles/2004/05/09/power_turns_good_soldiers_into_bad_apples/。

2. 奥利维亚·穆尔海德-斯劳特："道德和国家安全",《心理监控》, 2006 年 4 月, 登录日期 2015 年 9 月 17 日, http://www.apa.org/monitor/apr06/security.aspx。

3. 苏珊·T. 菲斯克, L. T. 哈里斯和 A. J. 卡迪："社会心理学: 为什么普通人会折磨敌人俘虏",《科学》第 306 卷, 2004 年第 5701 期, 第 1482—1483 页。

4. 菲斯克等: "普通人", 第 1482 页。

5. 小约翰·H. 库什曼: "五角大楼领导人因虐囚事件受到外界专家小组指责",《纽约时报》, 2004 年 8 月 24 日, 登录日期 2015 年 9 月 17 日, http://www.nytimes.com/2004/08/24/politics/24CND-ABUS.html。

6. 库什曼: "五角大楼领导人因虐囚事件受到外界专家小组指责"。

7. 津巴多: "权力将好士兵变成'坏苹果'"。

8. 菲利普·津巴多:《路西法效应: 好人是如何变成恶魔的》, 纽约: 兰登书屋, 2007 年, 第 370 页。

9. 津巴多:《路西法效应》, 第 370 页。

10. 津巴多:《路西法效应》, 第 371 页。

4 作者贡献

要点 🔑

- 在《路西法效应》一书中，津巴多试图通过他 1971 年斯坦福监狱实验中的证据和阿布格莱布监狱的虐囚事件来阐明情境的力量。

- 津巴多能够接触到斯坦福监狱实验和阿布格莱布监狱的所有相关数据，这在之前是未曾有过的，这让他能够进行其他人无法进行的比较研究。

- 苏珊·T.菲斯克和其他社会心理学家也在宣传"情境决定论者"这一思想流派，这一流派认为情境往往是导致普通人做出邪恶行为的原因。

作者目标

在《路西法效应》中，菲利普·津巴多意图提供证据和理论指导来探讨某些情境何时、如何以及为何会导致普通人做出令人震惊的施虐和邪恶行为。这一探讨不仅面向学界人士，也面向普通大众。

为了证实他的理论观点，津巴多详细描述了他 1971 年的斯坦福监狱实验。然后他列举了一些近期的历史事件，尤其是 2003 年美军入侵伊拉克时在阿布格莱布监狱发生的虐囚丑闻来作为证据。这些案例和斯坦福监狱实验有着特殊的关联。这两起事件都是在监狱环境中发生的；在这两起案例中，狱卒侮辱囚犯，剥夺囚犯的睡眠，从精神上控制囚犯，这些虐待行为让人始料未及。当然，阿布格莱布的狱卒还实施性虐待和肉体折磨，令人发指。

自斯坦福监狱实验以来的这些年，津巴多一直在描述和宣传情境因素。而在本书中，津巴多扩展了他的论点。关于《路西法效应》，他写道："如果我在斯坦福监狱实验结束后马上就写这本书，我可能会很乐意去详述情境因素是如何展现出一种超越我们想象的强大力量的……（但是）我可能会只看到冰山一角而错过更重要的东西，那是让好人为恶的一股更为强大的力量——系统的力量。"[1]

《路西法效应》一书中，津巴多将目光投向了更高层次——大规模的系统，如政府、文化或组织机构，它们为危险的情境创造了可能的条件，而这些情境接下来又会引发邪恶。

津巴多写这本书的最后一个重要目的是要研究并分享人们如何能够避免受到情境和系统因素的影响，而不至于被推向邪恶。在阿布格莱布虐囚事件的早期报告发布以后，苏珊·T.菲斯克及其合著者希望社会心理学能够更好地理解人们何时以及为何不屈从于情境压力。菲斯克于2004年在《科学》杂志中写道："对类似阿布格莱布虐囚事件的罪恶行为的解释揭示了一些能够有助于避免这些事件发生的科学原理。"[2]津巴多注意到了这一呼声，针对如何有效规避容易导致施虐行为的情境压力，他在《路西法效应》中专门匀出篇幅提出了一些解决办法。

> "阿布格莱布监狱的虐囚事件和斯坦福监狱实验中发生的一系列事情存在一些相似之处，这使我们在斯坦福监狱的经历更有说服力。反过来，它又揭示了在真实监狱环境中造成可怕虐囚行为的心理动因。"
> ——菲利普·津巴多：《路西法效应：好人是如何变成恶魔的》

研究方法

　　津巴多利用斯坦福监狱实验的数据，证明了强大的情境力量会导致普通人作恶。在《路西法效应》中，他对斯坦福监狱实验进行了详尽的描述，包括之前未曾发表的有关该实验的详尽的文字记录和录像片段的描述。

　　在军事法庭（军事审判）中，津巴多以专家证人的身份为在阿布格莱布监狱中实施虐囚行为的前中士伊万·弗里德里克作证，并享有特权，可以自由地调用各种资料。津巴多在《路西法效应》中描述了他如何获得了对这个案件的全面了解。"与其说我是社会心理学家，还不如说我是一名新闻调查记者。"[3]他写道："从对这个年轻人的深度采访，到和（了解他的人）谈话以及书信联系，我试图揭开有关他的一切真相⋯⋯ 我有权查阅所有记录暴行的数码影像，一共有好几百份⋯⋯（并且）还给我提供了所有当时可以从各种军事和民间调查委员会获取的报告。"[4]根据这些数据，津巴多得以提供了一份迄今为止最为详尽的报告，描述了情境因素是如何导致斯坦福监狱实验和阿布格莱布监狱中一些虐囚行为和酷刑的发生，这其中许多情境因素在大多数监狱中都存在。

　　这两个情境由于类似的监狱动态环境而具有可比性。然而，津巴多也讨论了自斯坦福监狱实验以来的几十年内的其他真实案例，在这些案例中，情境引发了罪恶行为。这些案例包括美国能源公司安然腐败案和 1994 年卢旺达的种族灭绝，后者导致占人口少数的图西族中多达 100 万人被屠杀，以及世界各地罗马天主教会的神职人员犯下的性侵案。在这些不同的案例中，津巴多证明了引发这些事件的是众多相同的情境解释和群体压力，其中包括归属 * 社会群体的需求（社会心理学家认为希望为他人所接受是人类的基本需求）和一旦加入群体就必须承受的从众压力（通过改变自己，以适应群体中大家的共同思维过程和行为方式）。

时代贡献

自 20 世纪 60 年代以来，菲利普·津巴多、斯坦利·米尔格拉姆和其他心理学家都一直是情境力量的支持者，他们认为情境因素会影响行为，并经常超越性情因素如内在的人格特质带来的影响。这一"情境决定论者"的思想流派已被广泛接受，它尤其可以用来解释处于新奇和令人紧张的情境中的人们的行为。

对于阿布格莱布监狱的许多看守而言，"新奇的和令人紧张的"这两种情境都是真实的——他们刚刚被派驻到监狱，而后又被迫平息大量监狱骚乱，与此同时，他们还要面临外部势力入侵监狱的威胁。2004 年，菲斯克和她的合著者写道："实际上，如果被激怒、被施压、感到不满或情绪激动到了一定程度，人人都可能表现出攻击性。部署在阿布格莱布监狱看守因犯的第 800 宪兵旅所处的情境正好符合所有已知会引发攻击行为的社会条件。"[5]

这个学派的思想很大程度上是基于米尔格拉姆和津巴多于 20 世纪 60 年代和 70 年代开展的重大研究。从某种程度来说，津巴多在《路西法效应》中主要帮助现代读者回顾了自己建立的思想体系，并且凭借几十年来收集的最新证据让自己的思想更具有时代性。

1. 菲利普·津巴多：《路西法效应：好人是如何变成恶魔的》，纽约：兰登书屋，2007年，第x页。

2. 苏珊·T.菲斯克、L.T.哈里斯和A.J.卡迪："社会心理学：为什么普通人会折磨敌人俘虏"，《科学》第306卷，2004年第5701期，第1483页。

3. 津巴多：《路西法效应》，第ix页。

4. 津巴多：《路西法效应》，第ix—x页。

5. 菲斯克等："普通人"，第1483页。

第二部分：学术思想

5 思想主脉

- 在《路西法效应》中，菲利普·津巴多认为，当处于特定情境或系统因素的压力下，几乎每个人都可能做出不道德或邪恶的行为。

- 斯坦福监狱实验证明了看似正常的人也可能会施虐——也就是说，从残暴的行为中获得快感。同时，津巴多认为阿布格莱布监狱中也存在类似的情境和系统因素。

- 在书中，津巴多使用隐喻总结了他的主题思想，生动详细地重述了斯坦福监狱实验，告诉了大家普通人也有可能变成恶魔。

核心主题

在《路西法效应》中，菲利普·津巴多审视了外部力量的影响，它会"让我们表现反常、破坏力强、邪恶无比"。[1] 他没有给邪恶行为下定义，也没有限定邪恶行为的范围。他认为，外部力量可以导致邪恶行为。事实上，尽管"邪恶"这一概念在书中十分重要，但他却没给他认为的"邪恶"下定义，而是列举此类行为的案例，集中讨论发生在斯坦福监狱实验和阿布格莱布监狱中的虐囚事件。

津巴多的分析始终贯穿着两个关键的主题思想：

- 首先，善与恶是可以互相渗透的（在这个案例中意指可以互相转换）。津巴多的意思是，"天使也可以变成魔鬼……魔鬼也可以变成天使。"[2] 所以，大多数人都具备两者的潜质。

- 其次，世间的许多罪恶应更多归因于外部因素，而非性情因素（即个体的人格）。津巴多认为存在着一种影响等级，系统因素（如政府、组织机构或文化）是罪恶的源头，然后是情境力量，最后才是性情。

当谈到第二个主题时，津巴多重新定义了习语——"一些坏苹果"。这个传统习语的意思是每一桶苹果中至少会有几个坏苹果。它的比喻义是说一群人中当然会有几个害群之马。在津巴多看来，这个比喻的存在就证明了人们倾向于认为邪恶行为的根本原因是个体内在的性情。但他说，"像这种'坏苹果性情论'忽略了苹果桶及其对苹果可能产生的腐化作用。"[3]

津巴多觉得分析更应该聚焦于"木桶的制造者，即有权力设计木桶的人"。[4] 他提出了用更符合事实的"坏木桶"比喻来代替"坏苹果"这个传统的习语。津巴多写道，"木桶的制造者"几乎可以包括任何一个有权操控情境和影响行为的人：政府、公司领导、体育教练、部队长官、宗教领袖甚至身为斯坦福监狱实验首席实验者的津巴多自己。

> "斯坦福监狱实验得到的一个主要结论是：一系列情境因素形成了不易察觉的普遍性力量，对个体的抵抗意志产生了压倒性影响。"
>
> —— 菲利普·津巴多：《路西法效应：好人是如何变成恶魔的》

思想探究

津巴多核心主题背后的许多思想和证据均来源于斯坦福监狱实验。在 1971 年开展的这项实验中，津巴多在斯坦福大学心理学系的地下室搭建了一个临时监狱，并随机给 24 名年轻的男性志愿者分配角色，或当囚犯，或当狱卒，而津巴多则扮演典狱长的角色。他写道，随机给参与者分配狱卒的角色"确保了他们一开始是好苹果，是在进入坏木桶，也就是这座监狱以后才被潜移默化的力量所腐蚀。"[5]

换句话说，囚犯和狱卒在实验开始之前都是可以互换角色的。这些狱卒掌权后，仅仅基于他们被随机分配到的角色，很快就开始辱骂囚犯，强迫他们干体力活，故意干扰他们的睡眠，并且将其中一些人隔离起来，实施单独监禁 *。

实验原计划进行两个星期，但是津巴多在第一周结束时就中止了实验，因为几名犯人在遭受了狱卒对他们实施的生理和心理虐待后感到十分痛苦。津巴多在《路西法效应》中概述了这种虐待对囚犯的影响，他写道："一半的学生犯人因为严重的情感和认知障碍而不得不被提前释放。"[6]

津巴多将这个实验的结果用于分析发生在阿布格莱布监狱的虐囚和酷刑事件，并声称监狱中发生的一切和之前在斯坦福监狱实验中的情形类似，只是更为残暴而已。津巴多认为，这两起事件都是由情境和系统因素造成的。

津巴多描述了这两种环境下许多类似的情境因素。他说，"无聊和厌倦在两种环境下都起了作用，"[7]看守没有受过正规训练，他们拥有绝对权力，但是却几乎不承担任何责任。在谈到更广泛的系统性因素时，津巴多认为伊拉克战争 * 期间存在着一种美国政府和军方助长的"虐待文化"[8]。他写道，他们用"美丽的言辞包装酷刑，却未能提供必要的领导、监督、问责和任务特训。"[9]比如，美国政府官员将入侵伊拉克定性为"反恐战争"[10]的一部分，他们使用"优化的审讯方式"这一术语来代替酷刑。在津巴多看来，这些政策可能会促使人们将虐待伊拉克战俘的行为视为正常的，甚至是合理的。

语言表述

津巴多使用比喻和习语来说明他的一些主题思想。这方面最突出的一个例子就是他对"坏苹果"的比喻进行了重新表述并以此引入了"坏木桶"的概念。另一个例子是书名——《路西法效应》，津巴多从基督教神话中引用了路西法 * 的故事。路西法原是上帝的天使，代表一切善和道德，但他之后却失去了上帝的恩宠，堕落成最可怕的恶魔。津巴多问他的读者："我们是否会像上帝最爱的天使路西法一样，不能抵制诱惑而对他人做出可怕之事？"[11] 津巴多的答案很明确是肯定的。路西法的故事恰如其分地表现了这种道德转变。尽管这些例子有些简单化，但它们是理解津巴多主题思想的切入点，也是对其主题思想的总结。

津巴多用了大量篇幅描述 1971 年的斯坦福监狱实验。他认为这些描述是"各章节按时间顺序记录……以电影的形式呈现，如同有一位旁白讲述一个正在上演的故事，并辅之以少许心理学方面的解释。"[12] 结果，这一部分相较于书中其他部分少了一些学术性，而多了一点戏剧性。

津巴多还将实验录像的文字稿和实验后的采访写入书中，这为他的许多主张提供了富有洞察力的证据。一位被指定为狱卒的参与者描述了他的经历："我以折磨和惩罚囚犯为乐，这其实不是我的天性，因为我认为我会同情伤者，特别是动物。我想，正是因为我可以完全自由地管理犯人，我才开始滥用权力。"[13] 这位参与者的经历触及了津巴多所倡导的主题：在强大的情境中，人们的行为会发生重大转变，这种转变往往是出人意料的，甚至可能是恶毒残暴的。

1. 菲利普·津巴多：《路西法效应：好人是如何变成恶魔的》，纽约：兰登书屋，2007 年，第 vii 页。
2. 津巴多：《路西法效应》，第 3 页。
3. 津巴多：《路西法效应》，第 10 页。
4. 津巴多：《路西法效应》，第 10 页。
5. 津巴多：《路西法效应》，第 229 页。
6. 津巴多：《路西法效应》，第 196 页。
7. 津巴多：《路西法效应》，第 352 页。
8. 津巴多：《路西法效应》，第 377 页。
9. 津巴多：《路西法效应》，第 378 页。
10. 津巴多：《路西法效应》，第 378 页。
11. 津巴多：《路西法效应》，第 xii 页。
12. 津巴多：《路西法效应》，第 xii 页。
13. 津巴多：《路西法效应》，第 187 页。

6 思想支脉

要点 🔑

- 《路西法效应》的思想支脉包括审视使人变坏的心理和社会机制，以及津巴多为避开这些陷阱而提出的一些建议。

- 津巴多将群体因素描述为将人们引向邪恶的机制，包括希望被群体接纳的心理渴望以及群体中匿名感的影响。一个人想要成为英雄，就必须意识到这些因素，并与之做斗争。

- 在书中，他还提出了一个新的想法：必须审视更广泛的系统通常是如何滋生诱发邪恶的各种情境的。同时，他也讨论了这些因素是如何相对受到忽视的。

其他思想

菲利普·津巴多的《路西法效应》包含两条思想支脉：

- 一套把人们推向邪恶深渊的特定的心理和社会机制。他详述了他认为的最重要的机制。
- 通过有意识地抵抗这些因素，人们可以成为英雄——"当某些人正在作恶或对恶行无动于衷时，代表他人挺身而出。"[1]

津巴多利用 50 年来的社会心理学研究成果来寻找致使人们犯罪的心理和社会机制，最后他得出结论：有两组不同类别的因素导致犯罪。第一组可被视为基于群体的因素，如归属感和被群体接纳的需求。当至少有两个人的时候，这些群体因素就会存在，其中一人或多人对群体中的其他人施加影响，如同辈压力*。当谈到这些群体性因素产生的影响时，津巴多指出："一想到有可能会被踢

（出圈子），人们实际上就会无所不用其极，只要能够避免被排挤出局这一可怕局面。"[2]

第二组可以认为是匿名因素，津巴多解释道，这是"任何让人自感匿名的事情或情境，好像没有人知道他们是谁或者想要了解他们是谁。"[3]他接着说，这些因素的影响降低了人们的"个人责任感，进而成为邪恶的温床。"[4]互联网上的交流证明了这种影响，这种交流经常是匿名的，通常较之于面对面交流少了些礼貌，而多了些敌意。

津巴多另一条思想支脉是，人们可以像英雄一样避开这些陷阱。津巴多不但认为大多数人都有能力作恶，他也认为大多数人都能够成为英雄。当津巴多谈到"普通人"可能以一种常见的方式作"恶"时，他写道："平庸之恶*与平庸之壮举有很多相似之处。两者都不能归因于独一无二的性情倾向。"[5]换句话说，一个人的个性未必和他为恶或为善的能力有太大关系。相反，津巴多认为，英雄能够成功地规避诱发许多人为恶的群体和匿名因素。

> "在'平庸之恶'的概念里，普通人要对他们同伴最残酷、最堕落的卑鄙行为负责，而我主张'平庸之壮举'，它让那些随时愿意在关键时刻尽人性本分的男男女女高举英雄行为的大旗。"
>
> —— 菲利普·津巴多：《路西法效应：好人是如何变成恶魔的》

思想探究

在津巴多看来，可能诱发恶行的第一类机制是群体性心理因素。他认为归属感是一个重要的机制，正是这种心理需求导致了斯坦福监狱实验的结果。他写道："想要有归属感，想要与人交往，想要为他人接受，这对于营造集体和家庭纽带太重要了。但这些基本需求在斯坦福监狱实验中却被用于迫使人们遵从新规范*，从而助长了狱卒们虐待囚犯的行为。"[6] 在心理学领域，"规范"指的是在任何一个特定的群体中业已接受的或人们期待的标准、价值观以及行为和思维方式，它由群体自身来确定。通过这种方式，津巴多解释了这一现象：人们有时候愿意放弃自己的道德本性，以此来换取一个他们有意或必须加入的团体的认可。

在《路西法效应》中，津巴多也考虑了其他群体性因素，如从众和对权威的服从。他提到心理学家斯坦利·米尔格拉姆于20世纪60年代开展的服从权威研究*，证明了权威在说服他人服从命令方面影响巨大。在这些实验中，实验者要求受试者对作答错误的陌生人实施模拟电击。尽管被电击者提出抗议，但是大多数受试者都实施了最大强度的电击。总体来说，这些群体因素都涉及到一个强有力的领导者或者群体规范，这些会影响群体成员的行为，使其违背自己的道德标准。

津巴多说的第二组能够引发邪恶的机制是匿名的因素。"去个性化"*是一种心理现象，人们在一个大的群体中会产生一种匿名感，以至于他们会失去自我意识和个人责任感，从而导致一些原本不符合个性的行为。

另一方面，去人性化*包括故意忽视或贬低其他人（或群体）的人性，经常将其视为次要的、低人一等的，甚至就像动物一样。正如津巴多所描述的，去人性化就是将另一些人"从身为人类一员的道德秩序中排除"。[7] 他指出，在引发邪恶的情境中，这两个进程往往发挥了作用。比如说，在斯坦福监狱实验中，狱卒用编号而非名字呼叫犯人，这抹杀了后者的人性。同时，狱卒们自己戴着反光太阳镜，穿着制服，让自己也失去个性。

关于英雄，津巴多写道，他们并没有"神赐的天生善良，而是更可能在直觉上深知心理和社会的抵抗策略。"[8] 因此，正如津巴多认为几乎每个人都可能作恶一样，他也同样认为几乎每个人都可能成为英雄。但是，要想成为英雄，就必须意识到把人们引向邪恶的心理和社会影响，并且找到办法摆脱它们。比如说，对你的作为或不作为有所认识，并且有意识地对其负责，就会有助于抵抗导致去个性化的情境影响。

被忽视之处

尽管《路西法效应》是一本相对较新的著作（2007年出版），但是其中许多研究成果和观点都来自津巴多等人的早期研究工作。然而，津巴多承认他和该领域的同事之前忽略了系统（意指更大的组织机构、政府和文化）在引发邪恶方面的心理影响，因而没有能够探究影响每种情境的深层次力量。

当谈到更大的系统时，津巴多写道，"政治、经济、宗教、历史和文化框架能够定义情境，而大多数心理学家对其中蕴含的深层力量已经麻木了。"[9] 在他看来，他的学术同行们成功地审视了监狱、学校、教堂或个体的简单集合等情境对行为的影响。但是研究者们一直忽视了这些群体是如何在真实世界中产生的，也没有考虑到情境创造者所拥有的权力。

比如，在《路西法效应》中，津巴多特别谴责了美国总统乔治·W.布什*、副总统迪克·切尼*、国防部长唐纳德·拉姆斯菲尔德*和其他几位在阿布格莱布监狱虐囚事件中掌权的军队领导人。他指出，上述那些领导人帮助建立和培养了一种文化，这种文化催生了导致阿布格莱布监狱虐囚事件的"坏木桶"[10]。

以往，社会心理学家认为在系统层面进行分析通常超出了他们的研究领域，认为这些应该由社会学家（研究人类社会）、政治学家（研究政治体系的属性和行为以及体系中的参与者）和经济学家来完成。津巴多对系统层面的关注是《路西法效应》一书中较新的观点之一。因此，心理学家未来将在多大程度上考虑系统层面的变量——至少在审视诱发不道德行为的情境根源时——仍有待观察。

1. 菲利普·津巴多：《路西法效应：好人是如何变成恶魔的》，纽约：兰登书屋，2007年，第 viii 页。

2. 津巴多：《路西法效应》，第 259 页。

3. 津巴多：《路西法效应》，第 301 页。

4. 津巴多：《路西法效应》，第 301 页。

5. 津巴多：《路西法效应》，第 485 页。

6. 津巴多：《路西法效应》，第 258 页。

7. 津巴多：《路西法效应》，第 307 页。

8. 津巴多：《路西法效应》，第 xiii 页。

9. 津巴多：《路西法效应》，第 x 页。

10. 津巴多：《路西法效应》，第 x 页。

7 历史成就

要点 ⚷

- 在《路西法效应》中，菲利普·津巴多对斯坦福监狱实验进行了最为详尽的阐述和分析，并利用这一分析来解释阿布格莱布监狱丑闻中涉及的情境压力。
- 由于阿布格莱布监狱的虐囚事件以及津巴多所参与的针对其中一名监狱看守的审讯都是相对近期的事件，所以这本书合乎时宜，也有启示意义。
- 斯坦福监狱实验的可靠性及其调查结论的普遍性很难去证实，因为从道德角度考量，很大程度上难以复制最初的实验。

观点评价

在评论菲利普·津巴多的《路西法效应：好人是如何变成恶魔的》时，社会心理学家罗伯特·莱文问道："为什么这本新书讲述了一项35年前的实验？"[1]他自问自答："（津巴多）提供了大量新的诠释和新的材料——秘闻、囚犯和狱卒的日记、参与者的最新生活状况，他还记录了他的调查结果对真实世界中监狱政策所起到的影响。"[2]

这些例子包括津巴多直接提交给司法部门和执法部门的调查结果以及他在法庭上的证词——他认为将囚犯单独监禁是对囚犯的心理摧残和折磨。

尽管津巴多对英雄行为的分析和对系统因素（如政府）如何使强大的情境得以形成的分析在某种程度上还不够全面，但是这些分析却为后续深入研究提供了一个有价值的起点。津巴多在《路西法效应》中指出，社会心理学家在很大程度上忽视了英雄行为和系统对行为的影响等主题，他希望自己能够激发对这些主题的后续研究。莱文称赞了津巴多在英雄行为方面的研究和他对英雄思想和行为的精准定义和分类，同时他还说，他希望津巴多的研究"将会激励早就应该在这个领域开展的研究和教育"。[3]

尽管研究者们在很大程度上依旧忽视了这个话题，但津巴多正在尽自己所能让世界了解他的"英雄创想计划"，这项公共培训计划可以教人们如何规避潜在的隐患，从而展现英雄行为。这些隐患包括去个性化（由于从属于某个群体或因为匿名状态而失去自我意识和自我行为倾向）、去人性化（忽视或贬低他人的人类属性）和从众（因为社会压力等因素而迫使自己去顺从群体的思想和行为）。

> "凭借 20 世纪 70 年代斯坦福监狱实验中开创性的研究工作，津巴多出色地审视了当前阿布格莱布监狱的虐囚丑闻。好人为了满足天生对安全、知识和情感的正常需求，有时就被引向邪恶之途，津巴多细致地描述了促使好人作恶的情境因素。"
>
> —— 罗斯·麦克德莫特："津巴多著《路西法效应：好人是如何变成恶魔的》书评"

当时的成就

虽然斯坦福监狱实验已经过去 30 多年，但阿布格莱布监狱发生的事件深深地触动了津巴多，也使得重述这项实验比以往更具有现实意义和教育意义。在对《路西法效应》的书评中，政治学家罗斯·麦克德莫特说，"阿布格莱布监狱的照片公布以后，大约 30 年前的斯坦福监狱实验仍然与之具有强烈的关联性。"[4] 她指出这本书"包含了原始实验中的许多照片，这些照片冲击着每一位读者，实验中监狱看守命令囚犯们摆出的某些姿势，简直和最近公开的阿布格莱布监狱照片惊人地相似，性质和尺度简直如出一辙。"[5]

甚至连 2004 年施莱辛格报告——由美国国防部委托调查阿布格莱布虐囚事件的独立报告——都指出了两者的关联性。报告认为："斯坦福监狱实验具有里程碑意义，它给所有的军事拘留行动提供了警示。"[6] 考虑到施莱辛格报告的官方背景和媒体对此的大量关注，一些观察家们原本希望该报告能够影响美国对待外国战俘和恐怖嫌疑人的政策。然而，后来的报告（包括一份由一个专门保护政治犯人权的组织——大赦国际[*] 于 2010 年提供的报告）发现，在施莱辛格报告发布和《路西法效应》出版后，美国政府虐待和折磨被拘留者的现象在其他监狱又持续了若干年。不过，阿布格莱布监狱最终于 2008 年关闭。

局限性

心理学家斯坦利·米尔格拉姆的服从权威研究和津巴多的斯坦福监狱实验生动地揭示了可能存在的大量意想不到的邪恶行为。然而，由于道德因素的考量，这些实验都无法复制，因为它们都是将参与者置于在今天看来会对心理产生极大压力的场景之中，这种场景无法再现。因此，很难证实情境力量的普遍性。

社会心理学家还指出，人们对情境力量的感知程度因文化而异。津巴多在书中写道："传统的观点（持这一观点的人来自个人主义[*] 色彩浓厚的文化背景）是从内在寻找答案——病理学或英雄主义。现代精神病学倾向于性情论。"[7] 换句话说，在一些强调"个人主义"的文化中，如在美国等西方国家，人们往往将自己视为个体而非群体中的一员。因此，他们通常倾向于将事情的原因归结于先天的人格因素（即"性情"），所以，人们认为，一个人的攻击性行为很可能表明其本身就具有攻击性的人格，而不是某个情境因素造成的。

津巴多指出，对于是否采用"坏苹果"论去解释不道德行为，各文化看法不一，其中，美国和西方文化可能会更愿意归因于坏苹果。而在非西方文化中，如东亚，人们往往更能感知情境因素及其对他们生活的影响。至少在津巴多看来，这就导致在个人主义文化深厚的西方社会人们不太可能注意到并质疑可能会制造邪恶情境的当权者，比如他们的政府或老板。

该书的另一个不足之处在于津巴多不愿意给他认为的"邪恶"下定义，而是给出了很多他认为属于邪恶行径的事例，包括斯坦福监狱实验和阿布格莱布监狱中狱卒的行为、财务造假、种族大屠杀和性虐待等一系列案例。津巴多指出，他认为邪恶涉及的范围比他印象中人们通常描绘的更广泛。他写道，这绝不限于"那些精心策划大屠杀的政治领导者们"。[8] 津巴多似乎有意将邪恶视为一个界限不明的宽泛范畴。但他并没有在书中提及不同的人和不同的社会是否有可能对邪恶持不同的看法。

1. 罗伯特·莱文："人犯下的罪行"，《美国科学家》，2007 年 9—10 月，登录日期 2015 年 9 月 15 日，http://americanscientist.org/bookshelf/content2/2007/5/the-evil-that-men-do。

2. 罗伯特·莱文："人犯下的罪行"。

3. 罗伯特·莱文："人犯下的罪行"。

4. 罗斯·麦克德莫特："津巴多著《路西法效应：好人是如何变成恶魔的》书评"，第 645 页。

5. 麦克德莫特："书评"，第 645 页。

6. 菲利普·津巴多：《路西法效应：好人是如何变成恶魔的》，纽约：兰登书屋，2007 年，第 324 页。

7. 津巴多：《路西法效应》，第 7 页。

8. 津巴多：《路西法效应》，第 6 页。

8 著作地位

要点 ⚷

- 菲利普·津巴多的研究方向之一在于查明人们何时以及如何做出意料之外的举动。1971 年开展的斯坦福监狱实验和 2007 年出版的《路西法效应》一书中展现了看似寻常的人们做出邪恶行为的事例。

- 虽然津巴多基于斯坦福监狱实验的研究为情境力量奠定了原型，但是他的另一些研究更依赖于性情因素，即那些和个体人格相关的因素。

- 然而，《路西法效应》的出版再次引发了斯坦福监狱实验最初于 20 世纪 70 年代所激起的争论。因此，这本书又一次确立了津巴多在情境研究方面的声望。

定位

《路西法效应：好人是如何变成恶魔的》于 2007 年出版。虽然这已经是津巴多职业生涯的后期，但因为涉及津巴多职业生涯早期的实验，这本书又重新回到了和作者关联最紧密的研究课题：情境力量、邪恶行为以及监禁的相互作用和心理后果。《路西法效应》一书中较新的内容包括：津巴多考虑到系统因素，并关注如何通过避免消极的情境力量来促发英雄行为。

津巴多在书中承认，在他职业生涯的大部分时期，他都忽视了诸如制度这样的系统力量。在一次采访中，他指出，他"甚至在斯坦福监狱实验中都没有意识到系统的力量，因为我本人就是系统。"[1] 他说，他在 2004 年以专家证人身份为因在阿布格莱布监狱中虐待被拘押者而受到指控的美国士兵伊万·弗里德里克出庭作证时才意识到这一点。

最重要的是，《路西法效应》标志着津巴多转向了他最关注的英雄行为。尽管他在书中只花了少量篇幅来探讨英雄行为，但这却为他后期对英雄行为的关注奠定了基础。2010 年，津巴多发起了"英雄创想计划"，帮助培训对此感兴趣的参与者来抵制消极的情境因素。他写道，这关键"在于三种力量：自我意识力、情境敏感力和世事洞察力"。[2] 所有这些需要首先理解消极情境因素的力量，如去个性化和从众，然后思考如何应对这些压力。因此，津巴多的"英雄创想计划"可以在《路西法效应》中找到其源头。

> "我对人性的转变最感兴趣。是什么让我们突然发生转变，是什么让我们不按照以往的行为方式或对自己和他人的了解行事？"
>
> —— 菲利普·津巴多访谈，见克里斯蒂娜·马斯拉奇：《边缘皇帝》

整合

尽管津巴多和斯坦福监狱实验以及"情境决定论"学派（关注情境的力量）关系密切，但他在整个职业生涯中涵盖了一系列的研究课题。事实上，他认为自己是心理学领域的通才，而非某个方面的专家。尽管如此，一些宽泛的主题贯穿了他的主要作品。

在一次采访中，他这样描述了自己的核心研究方向："一直以来，我主要关注普通人是如何以及为何会做出不同寻常的事情，这些事情似乎完全背离了他们的本性。"[3] 他另外两个重要研究方向是害羞和时间观念。在有关害羞的研究中，津巴多努力帮助害羞的人克服自卑心理，在某种意义上，就是以对他们来说不同寻常的方式表现自己。然而，与在《路西法效应》和其他关于邪恶的研究中的立场相反，津巴多对害羞的研究往往更关注性情。他将害羞看作一种人格变量，或者思维方式的结果，而不仅仅受到情境因素的影响。

津巴多对时间观念的研究也表明了他研究工作的多样性。它详细分析了一个人如果强调或者过于强调过去发生的事情、将来的可能性或现在的生活，那么他的行为将会受到什么样的影响。这就是心理学家所说的互动主义，因为它认为一个人的人格和情境之间的相互作用比单独的人格或情境因素更能预测一个人的行为。

津巴多明确表达了他对时间观念的这种看法，他写道，他认为时间观念"由情境决定，且是一个相对稳定的因个体差异而不同的过程。"[4]（简而言之，他认为情境和性情因素对形成时间观念都不可或缺。）因此，尽管津巴多的情境决定论立场在有关斯坦福监狱实验的著作和《路西法效应》中显而易见，但他在社会心理学方面的研究则更加多样化且细致入微，既包含性情方面的思想，也包含互动主义观点。

意义

津巴多凭借其特殊身份接触了两次重大事件，所以，《路西法效应》可能是他写的内容最广泛、描述最详细、阅读人数最多的一本著作。较之于他之前的著作，这本书主要针对美国军方和政府，不仅提出了更多批评意见，也提供了更多解决方案。例如，津巴多特别指责了美国前总统乔治·W.布什和前国防部长唐纳德·拉姆斯菲尔德，因为他们帮助建立的大规模系统最终让伊拉克人去人性化（也就是说，剥夺了他们作为人类的地位）。

《路西法效应》进一步强化了津巴多和斯坦福监狱实验的关联，也巩固了他作为情境决定论者的地位。自 20 世纪 70 年代津巴多开展斯坦福监狱实验以来，这种关联和他的身份便一直饱受争议。这本书的面世又重新激起了一些争论，让津巴多再次成为公众关注的焦点，对他的看法也呈现出两极分化。尽管斯坦福监狱实验在该领域被认为是最著名、最有趣、可能最具有教育意义的研究之一，但它也被视为最不道德的研究之一。津巴多在其职业生涯中多次承认这一点，包括在《路西法效应》中，他提出了这样一个问题："斯坦福监狱实验有违道德吗？从几个方面来看，答案是肯定的。"5

然而，津巴多对他的观点进行了补充说明，他认为如果以其他标准来衡量，这项研究并没有违反道德准则。他还声称，设想中斯坦福监狱实验参与者所承受的痛苦是可以接受的，也是有价值的。虽然这本书为该领域的一项重要研究提供了新的细节以及关于系统因素和英雄行为的新观点，但它同时也将津巴多推回到该领域有关道德之争的漩涡之中。在一些观察家看来，这势必会影响津巴多的声誉。

---

1. 玛丽娜·克拉科夫斯基："自由的津巴多"，《斯坦福杂志》，2007 年 5/6 月，登录日期 2015 年 9 月 27 日，https://alumni.standford.edu/get/page/magazine/article/?article_id=32541。

2. 菲利普·津巴多:《路西法效应: 好人是如何变成恶魔的》, 纽约: 兰登书屋,
2007 年, 第 452 页。

3. 克里斯蒂娜·马斯拉奇:"边缘皇帝",《今日心理学》, 2000 年 9 月 1 日, 登录
日期 2015 年 9 月 15 日, https://psychologytoday.com/articles/200009/emperor-the-edge。

4. 菲利普·G.津巴多和约翰·N.博伊德:"客观看待时间: 一个有效且可靠的衡
量个体差异的维度",《人格和社会心理学杂志》第 77 卷, 1999 第 6 期, 第
1272 页。

5. 津巴多:《路西法效应》, 第 231 页。

第三部分：学术影响

9 最初反响

要点 🗝

- 斯坦福监狱实验作为津巴多《路西法效应》中的主要内容,长期以来一直被指有违道德,而且研究方法也令人生疑。

- 津巴多承认斯坦福监狱实验在具体操作中有道德层面的过失;然而,面对研究方法上的批判,津巴多坚决捍卫最初的研究分析报告。

- 斯坦福监狱实验成为该领域伦理学方面研究的一个具有重大意义的案例。2007年出版的《路西法效应》更是重新引发了人们对津巴多为该研究结果所做解释的争论。

批评

因为菲利普·津巴多的《路西法效应:好人是如何变成恶魔的》在很大程度上有赖于斯坦福监狱实验,所以对这本书的批评也大多反映了针对这项1971年实验的最初批评,而且往往集中在两大要点:研究是否违反道德、研究方法是否正确。1973年,一位评论家特别针对该研究的伦理问题提出了批判,他声称,参与者在同意参加实验之前并未被告知准确的信息,并且他们也不应该受到折磨。

将近40年后,一位《路西法效应》的评论家指出,斯坦福监狱实验"现在被用来作为一项研究伦理走向歧途的案例"。[1]津巴多的斯坦福监狱实验参与者忍受的心理折磨超过了大多数社会学家认为可以接受的范围。批评者还认为,津巴多自己充当临时监狱的典狱长，因而他无法客观地监控参与者的状况和安全。

斯坦福监狱实验后的最初几年，对其研究方法的批评集中于对所发生事件的不同解释。许多人认为实验参与者的行为并不像津巴多所说的那样是有机统一的。常见的一种批评来自政治学家阿里·巴努阿齐齐＊和社会学家＊赛玛卡·穆瓦赫迪＊。他们在1975年写道，需求特性＊是导致斯坦福监狱实验中发生的一系列事件的主要原因。

"需求特性"这一术语指的是在某一情境中参与者对实验目的或者实验者的期望形成自己的理解。因此，他们感受到一种潜在的压力，要求他们按照预期的方式行事，他们便会下意识地改变自己的行为以和自己的理解保持一致。这样一来，结果就会产生偏差，也会让人们对观察结果的有效性产生质疑。

巴努阿齐齐和穆瓦赫迪认为，参与者可能已经觉察到了津巴多对这项研究的假设和期望，他们会调整自己的行为以满足他的愿望。巴努阿齐齐和穆瓦赫迪指出："受试者在参与实验时，对于在真实监狱中狱卒和囚犯的行为方式以及彼此之间的关系存在强烈的模式化观念，"[2] 并且他们基本上都是在扮演这一类角色。

> "斯坦福监狱实验研究不道德吗？不对，也对。说不对，是因为它经过人类受试者研究审查委员会＊的审核和批准，并且遵循了该委员会的指导原则……说对，是因为参与者遭受了痛苦，而一些人也被批准可以在很长一段时间内对其同伴们施加折磨和羞辱。"
> —— 菲利普·津巴多等："斯坦福监狱实验反思：开端、转变、结果"

回应

自《路西法效应》出版以来，津巴多似乎一直避免公开回应此类批评。针对有人对这本书的结论表示担忧或者对斯坦福监狱实验的方法有新疑虑这种情况，他于 2007 年在其个人网站上发布了一篇短文予以回应："我没有时间也没有兴趣对这个问题进行进一步的讨论或争论。"[3] 他可能认为再重申他前些年已经表明的立场没有意义，特别是《路西法效应》已经涵盖了他对这些批评的最初回应。

比如，津巴多早在 1973 年就承认这项研究在某些方面有违道德。但他也从几个方面为自己辩护。他提出，他开展此项研究之前已经获得了几个机构审查委员会 * 的批准。他还表示，他曾多次向参与者询问情况 *（在研究结束后的讨论中，向参与者提供更多有关这项研究的信息，并检查他们是否有心理压力）。津巴多指出，他揭示了实验的真实意图，并且"充分相信我们观察到的并应对之负责的痛苦可以解释为与刺激密切相关（也就是说，受到某个特定的刺激而产生某个特定行为），所以，痛苦只局限于地下监狱之中，没有扩散到其他地方。"[4]

津巴多在《路西法效应》中重申了这些观点，他说，虽然从绝对意义上来说，这项研究违反道德，但我们却从中了解到了足够的信息，这证明它给参与者施加的巨大压力是值得的。津巴多宣称："从有关道德争论的相对层面来看（也就是说，从代价和收益的相对价值来看，而不是基于绝对的事实和价值观做判断），可以说，斯坦福监狱实验并非违背道德标准。"[5]

津巴多在书中承认，的确可能存在某些需求特性。他写到了自己在研究中扮演的角色，指出："回想起来，我从富有同情心的老师转变为只关注数据的研究者，再到冷酷无情的典狱长，这种角色转换非常痛苦。"[6]

然而，津巴多提供了一种不同的解释。他认为这只是进一步证明了情境的力量，因为这项研究甚至都改变了他自己，而并非证明他或参与者是故意扮演角色。

冲突与共识

1971 年的斯坦福监狱实验很快招致批评，而且这种批评一直持续到《路西法效应》出版甚至以后的时间，对此，津巴多一直坚持自己对斯坦福监狱实验调查结论的最初解释，并对有关该研究道德方面的质疑保持始终如一的态度。而津巴多的批评者们似乎也并未动摇。他们将斯坦福监狱实验和斯坦利·米尔格拉姆在 20 世纪 60 年代开展的服从权威实验看作社会心理学领域违反道德准则的最佳范例。

2012 年出版了一本很有影响的关于研究伦理方面的手册，在书中，心理学家琼·E. 西贝尔*和社会学家马丁·B. 托里奇*认为："津巴多的道德问题源于……（他的）利益冲突，一方面他是研究者……另一方面他又是以典狱长的身份成为受试者中的一员。"[7] 他们写道，斯坦福监狱实验很有教育意义，这意味着："所有研究者都能从这种利益冲突中吸取教训。研究者……需要随时监控研究和受试者。"[8] 换句话说，他们认为，津巴多作为典狱长无法客观地监测实验参与者的安全。在这一点上，津巴多表示同意。

一直以来，斯坦福监狱实验研究中需求特性的作用饱受质疑，津巴多对实验分析的解释也面临挑战，不过人们还尚未达成共识。

津巴多继续维护他对斯坦福监狱实验的最初解释，同时将研究成果应用于对其他事件的分析，如阿布格莱布监狱虐囚事件。与此同时，《路西法效应》的出版也重新激发了人们的兴趣，他们试图为斯坦福监狱实验找到另一种解释。

---

1. 雷·赫伯特："邪恶的平庸性"，《观察家报》，2007 年 4 月，登录日期 2015 年 9 月 27 日，http://aps.psychologicalscience.org/index.php/publications/observer/2007/april-07/the-banality-of-evil.html。
2. 阿里·巴努阿齐齐和赛玛卡·穆瓦赫迪："模拟监狱中的人际动力学：方法分析"，《美国心理学家》第 30 卷，1975 年第 2 期，第 156 页。
3. 菲利普·津巴多："人、情境、系统的相互作用"，《路西法效应》，登录日期 2015 年 9 月 27 日，http://www.lucifereffect.com/apsrejoinder.htm。
4. 菲利普·G.津巴多："谈人类心理学研究的道德介入：从斯坦福监狱实验谈起"，《认知》第 2 卷，1973 年第 2 期，第 254 页。
5. 菲利普·津巴多：《路西法效应：好人是如何变成恶魔的》，纽约：兰登书屋，2007 年，第 263 页。
6. 津巴多：《路西法效应》，第 218 页。
7. 琼·E.西贝尔和马丁·B.托里奇：《道德责任的研究计划》，千橡：赛奇出版公司，2012 年，第 67 页。
8. 西贝尔和托里奇：《责任》，第 67 页。

10 后续争议

要点 🔑

- 《路西法效应》提出了论点和证据，证明了某些环境——如美国监狱——可能是滋生伤害、施虐和邪恶行为的温床。

- 《路西法效应》创立了一个学派，该学派认为恶劣的情境会使人变坏。另一派则针锋相对，认为是情境中的坏人让情境变得恶劣。

- 斯坦福监狱实验和《路西法效应》对监狱环境方面的研究影响尤为明显。

应用与问题

菲利普·津巴多的著作《路西法效应：好人是如何变成恶魔的》于 2007 年出版，书中的观点已经影响到了学界关于监狱管理政策的讨论。社会心理学家克雷格·哈尼 * 认为斯坦福监狱实验和其他监狱研究的证据表明："鉴于监狱的潜在危害性，在打击犯罪的过程中应该有节制地设置监狱。"[1] 哈尼是加利福尼亚大学圣克鲁兹分校的一位心理学教授，他因研究监禁造成的心理影响和监狱的有效性而闻名。他的核心观点是，如果像斯坦福监狱实验所揭示的那样，监狱能够改变人们的行为，那么这种力量应该用来改造囚犯。但是，正如斯坦福监狱实验和其他监狱研究描述的那样，监狱反而更有可能成为去人性化甚至从精神上摧残囚犯的地方。

尽管《路西法效应》影响了监狱管理政策，但它也同样引发了人们对津巴多的实验方法和斯坦福监狱实验解释的持续关注，而这种关注甚至在日益增加。2001 年，两位社会心理学家和心理学教授史蒂芬·赖歇尔 * 和 S. 亚历山大·哈斯拉姆 * 与英国广播公司（BBC）* 合作开展了一项著名的研究。研究者在一个临时拘留所随机将 15 名参与者分成囚犯和狱卒。但这并不是照搬斯坦福监狱实验，部分原因在于现代伦理学不允许这样做。在这个案例中，赖歇尔和哈斯拉姆报告说，"狱卒不愿施加他们的权威，甚至最后还被囚犯制服。"[2] 在研究的后续阶段，参与者试图建立平等的组织体系，实行平等主义 * 的原则，公平地分配任务以及日常工作。但这种方法最终失败了，取而代之的是重新建立一个狱卒—囚犯的等级制度。

> "监狱系统天然存在虐待犯人的可能性。作为一种实际监狱场景的全真模拟，无论有多少不足之处，斯坦福监狱实验仍然具有重要意义。它说明，无论何时对一群被贬损（被侮辱，被认为毫无价值）和被丑化的他者施行近乎绝对权力的时候，都有可能产生一种毁灭性的力量。"
>
> —— 克雷格·哈尼："伤害的文化：控制超高度戒备监狱里的残酷相互作用"

思想流派

BBC 的这项监狱研究 * 和关于斯坦福监狱实验的不同解释促使一个更加细分的研究情境力量的学派得以诞生。津巴多主张因果过程，认为恶劣的情境和系统（坏木桶）会生成坏苹果。但是 BBC 监狱实验表明如监狱这样的强大情境未必会如津巴多所言，堕入虐待和罪恶的深渊。

赖歇尔和哈斯拉姆认为，"强势群体成员的行为方式取决于与他们特定社会身份相关的规范和价值观，可能是反社会的，也可能是亲社会的。"[3] 这个论断在一定程度上表明，津巴多在斯坦福监狱实验中培育并创设了一种助长虐待的情境，并且对于斯坦福监狱实验的结果，津巴多本人要比他所详述的情境因素负更大的责任。

从进一步的研究来看，更有可能是"坏苹果"制造了"坏木桶"。2007年，心理学教授托马斯·卡纳汉*和山姆·麦克法兰*开展了一项研究，旨在调查那些应聘参与监狱研究的受试者的性格特征。他们发现，和应聘类似广告（省去"监狱生活"字眼）[4]来参与假设研究的人相比，"那些应聘一份明确提及要参与体验监狱生活的心理学研究的广告（这份广告几乎和斯坦福监狱实验的广告一模一样）的志愿者"[5]从多个维度而言往往具有更强的侵略性，且更倾向于支持权威和社会权势。

这一思想流派属于互动主义的类型，因为该学派不仅同样关注人格和情境因素对行为的决定作用，而且还认为，相较于单一的人格或情境因素，在特定情境中的特定人格间的相互作用能更好地预测行为。比如说，威权主义*人格的人——那些习惯于行使自身权威的人——处于像监狱一样等级森严的系统之中。

当代研究

除了这本书在社会心理学和人格心理学领域所引发的学术争论以外，津巴多以前的学生克雷格·哈尼（他也是斯坦福监狱实验期间的一个重要研究者）现在已经成为监狱研究和监狱政策制定领域的领军人物。哈尼在2008年写道："我们的社会以监禁的名义给犯人施加了巨大痛苦，我们已经承受不起由此带来的心理、社会、经济甚至是文化方面的代价了。"[6]他的这一结论源于过去几十年的研究，这些研究多数是从他参与斯坦福监狱实验时开始的，并且他的结论和津巴多对斯坦福监狱实验的分析以及给监狱政策制定带来的启示也基本一致。

哈尼发现在真实监狱中囚犯面临的心理压力和痛苦远比斯坦福监狱实验中更加严重。这种痛苦是由很多因素造成的，这些因素在斯坦福监狱实验中十分明显，如单独监禁囚犯、狱中滥用权力、强调监狱的惩罚功能而非改造功能等。

自 20 世纪 70 年代起，美国开始采取"'强硬'措施来控制犯罪"，[7] 包括扩大监狱规模、延长刑期等。哈尼写道，这些监狱的政策和做法已经"从施加痛苦跨越到了造成真正的伤害——无论从社会层面还是个人层面而言。"[8] 美国拘禁了大量罪犯，而没有去改造他们。在他们服刑期满重返社会之前，系统反而给他们带来了额外的心理伤害。

---

1. 克雷格·哈尼和菲利普·津巴多："美国监狱政策的过去和未来：斯坦福监狱实验后的 25 年"，《美国心理学家》第 53 卷，1998 年第 7 期，第 719 页。

2. 史蒂芬·赖歇尔和亚历山大·S.哈斯拉姆："专制心理学的再思考：BBC 监狱实验"，《英国社会心理学杂志》第 45 卷，2006 年第 1 期，第 1 页。

3. 赖歇尔和哈斯拉姆："专制"，第 33 页。

4. 托马斯·卡纳汉和山姆·麦克法兰："重温斯坦福监狱实验：参与者的自行选择造成了虐待吗？"，《人格和社会心理学公报》第 33 卷，2007 年第 5 期，第 610 页。

5. 卡纳汉和麦克法兰："重温"，第 610 页。

6. 克雷格·哈尼："对囚犯的战争的伤亡统计"，《旧金山大学法律评论》2008 年第 43 期，第 89 页。

7. 哈尼："囚犯"，第 88 页。

8. 哈尼："囚犯"，第 89 页。

11 当代印迹

要点 🔑

- 今天,《路西法效应》为著名的斯坦福监狱实验提供了最佳纪录。正是因为这本书,关于斯坦福监狱实验和情境力量在诱发不道德行为方面的争议再次爆发。菲利普·津巴多最近提出的有关行为和英雄主义的系统性原因的观点也源于这本书。

- 关于斯坦福监狱实验和情境力量的重新解读引发了持续的争议,但津巴多自那以后并未参与其中。相反,他将注意力转移到了新的研究之上,主要是关于英雄行为的研究。

- 社会心理学家和人格心理学家都继续对诱发不道德行为的情境力量展开争论。

地位

菲利普·津巴多的《路西法效应:好人是如何变成恶魔的》(2007)为1971年的斯坦福监狱实验提供了迄今为止最全面的描述和分析。正因为此,这部著作预计会在今后一段时间内对社会心理学领域产生历史意义。

书中有关斯坦福监狱实验的很多新信息也为双方辩论提供了新的素材。这包括之前未公开的研究记录、照片和录像片段描述。在一次研究后的采访中,一个狱卒对自己的行为感到惊讶,他说:"当一个囚犯对我反应过激的时候,我发现我不得不保护自己,那时我不是我,而是作为狱卒的我……他恨我这个狱卒,他对我的这身制服反应强烈。我别无选择,只能作为一名狱卒保护自己。"[1]

这些自我醒悟为津巴多的几个论点提供了佐证，比如人们对角色（这里是狱卒）的接受和他们去个性化的能力（在这里，狱卒暗示遭恨的不是"真实的自己"，而是"狱卒"）。

时至今日，对这本著作的大部分关注都集中于对情境力量的持续争论和对斯坦福监狱实验的不同解读之上。但目前有一些讨论将注意力集中于《路西法效应》中两个较新的话题之上。第一个是津巴多的主张：更庞大的系统导致了书中描写的各种恶劣情境的出现。第二个是津巴多对英雄行为的分析，他认为只有认识到并有能力避免恶劣情境的压力和陷阱，人们才能做出英雄的行为。

这些观点使津巴多有了一个新的定位，说明他已经逐渐脱离了早期的斯坦福监狱实验研究。这些见解不仅涉及到新的方案，而且还吸引了新的读者。政治学家＊罗斯·麦克德莫特在评价这本书时，将其总结为鼓励读者去抵制"政客等人的狡猾手段，他们利用环境操纵不知情的旁观者去为他们做坏事。"[2] 津巴多提倡的观点是，大家应该质疑政府的意图，这样做很有价值。

> "用'坏苹果'还是'坏木桶'来限定这个讨论是错误的。这个比喻过分简化了一个本来复杂且令人担忧的现实，那就是在很多地方都存在问题。"
> —— 乔治·R. 马斯特罗扬尼："回顾：理解阿布格莱布"

互动

津巴多一直是《路西法效应》中的观点的主要宣传者。近些年，他显然选择了不再参与到相关争论之中，这些争论涉及到他的研究方法以及情境因素在斯坦福监狱实验和阿布格莱布等事件中的作用程度。2007 年，津巴多在其个人网站上发表声明说，这些争论偏离了他希望在《路西法效应》中关注的因素。他写道："当人格心理学家和社会心理学家在为性情和情境的相对作用争论不休时，我们都忽略了行为倾向中最重要的因素，那就是系统。"[3]

所以，津巴多似乎正聚焦于《路西法效应》中的最新主题：系统对人类行为和英雄主义的影响。这是对社会心理学和人格心理学领域的最新挑战。津巴多认为对情境力量的研究已经很充分，他希望将工作重心转移到更加积极、更加实用的英雄行为研究上来。在2011 年的一篇文章中，他写道："什么让我们为善？什么让我们为恶？第二个问题的答案已经从上述研究中找到了……但是，如果我们问人何以成为英雄，还没有研究能够给出答案。"[4] 看来，在《路西法效应》之后，津巴多已经很快将注意力从预测邪恶转移到预测英雄行为上来了。

持续争议

然而，那些受到津巴多质疑的研究者们并没有放弃关于情境因素影响的争论。2007 年，数十位社会和人格心理学家（其中一些是全世界最德高望重的学者）给美国一个重要的心理研究机构心理科学协会*写了一封信，表达了对《路西法效应》的担忧。他们写道："与津巴多恰恰相反，我们相信，实际上几乎没有科学证据能表明情境因素比性情因素更能解释人们的行为。"[5] 他们还对津巴多用情境因素来解释发生在阿布格莱布监狱的虐囚事件提出了质疑。

同样，在对斯坦福监狱实验和斯坦利·米尔格拉姆的服从权威研究进行重新分析时，社会心理学家史蒂芬·赖歇尔和 S. 亚历山大·哈斯拉姆拍摄了一部由志愿者参加的纪录片并在英国广播公司播出，该纪录片对斯坦福监狱实验进行了重新解读。他们坚持认为大量调查研究并不支持"情境会导致大部分人为恶"这一观点。

赖歇尔和哈斯拉姆认为长期存在的"情境决定论"观点忽视了很多人确实抵制了津巴多所说的情境力量这一事实，并且认为那些屈从于情境压力的人"在听从权威而犯下恶行时是故意地而非盲目地，是主动地而非被动地，是创造性地而非机械地……简而言之，他们应被视作并被判定为积极的追随者而非盲目的服从者。"[6]因此，赖歇尔和哈斯拉姆认为，事实情况并非如津巴多所认为的那样，普通人受到情境影响而作恶，而是有作恶倾向的人会受到情境的影响。

1. 菲利普·津巴多：《路西法效应：好人是如何变成恶魔的》，纽约：兰登书屋，2007 年，第 189 页。

2. 罗斯·麦克德莫特："津巴多《路西法效应：好人是如何变成恶魔的》书评"，《政治心理学》第 28 卷，2007 年第 5 期，第 646 页。

3. 菲利普·津巴多："人、情境、系统的相互作用"，《路西法效应》，登录日期 2015 年 9 月 27 日，http://www.lucifereffect.com/apsrejoinder.htm。

4. 菲利普·津巴多："什么造就了英雄？"，《至善科学中心》，2011 年 1 月 18 日，登录日期 2015 年 9 月 27 日，http://greatergood.berkeley.edu/article/item/what_makes_a_hero/。

5. 布伦特·M. 唐纳伦等："不要太强调情境"，《观察家报》，2007 年 6/7 月，登录日期 2015 年 9 月 27 日，http://psychologicalscience.org/index.php/publications/observer/2007/june-july-07/not-so-situational.html。

6. 亚历山大·S. 哈斯拉姆和斯蒂芬·D. 赖歇尔："质疑从众的'天性'：米尔格拉姆和津巴多的研究真正说明了什么"，《美国科学公共图书馆：生物学》第 10 卷，2012 年第 11 期，第 1 页。

12 未来展望

要点 ⚷━━

- 《路西法效应》可能会继续引发有关人们如何解读斯坦福监狱实验和有关情境力量引发不道德行为方面的争议。然而，它未来也可能会激励对英雄行为的新研究。
- 在不远的将来，菲利普·津巴多很有可能通过英雄创想计划等任务来开展相关研究。
- 这本书之所以具有开创性，有很多原因，其中一个原因就是它生动而全面地再现了心理学领域最著名的一项研究。

潜力

菲利普·津巴多在 1971 开展的斯坦福监狱实验和 2007 年出版的《路西法效应：好人是如何变成恶魔的》一书将继续成为关于研究伦理的典型案例，也将是有关行为的情境决定因素这一争论中最受关注的部分。心理学教授乔治·R. 马斯特罗扬尼 * 写道："在对斯坦福监狱实验的几乎是以小时为单位的翔实记录中，心理学家会发现大量极有价值的新信息。"[1] 他还表示："通过提供新的信息，津巴多为该领域做出了突出贡献，这将有望促使人们重新思考斯坦福监狱实验带来的教训。"[2]

确实，这本书在面世几年内就重新引发了人们对斯坦福监狱实验的关注，甚至包括与之相关的斯坦利·米尔格拉姆的服从权威研究。虽然津巴多写作这本书的意图并不在于重新燃起这场争论，更何况他还对喋喋不休的争论表示失望，但是这场争论也让人们从一个更细微的角度来理解邪恶。

津巴多已经将他的思想应用在英雄行为研究之中，并且这项研究的规模可能会在未来几年中有所扩大。在早期的实践应用中，最主要的成就是他设立了一个非营利性组织——英雄创想计划，这个计划旨在"教人们如何采取有效行动去应对具有挑战性的情境"。[3]津巴多写道，这个项目意图开展和鼓励将来对英雄行为的研究，并向"初高中、公司和军队提供基于该研究的教育和培训项目，使人们意识到社会因素会产生被动性、消极性，激励他们采取主动积极的公民行动，并鼓励他们培养能够持续将展现英雄行为的冲动转化为实际行动的本领。"[4]

> "凭借对这些的深入了解，我开启了一个项目，旨在了解更多的英雄行为，创造更多的明日英雄。"
>
> —— 菲利普·津巴多："什么造就了英雄？"

未来方向

时至今日，津巴多仍然是致力于宣传情境力量的最直言不讳、最引人注目、成就最杰出的一位思想家——他强调情境力量能够导致普通人"为恶"，这就为历史上的种种暴行提供了解释。此外，他也有可能继续成为宣传英雄行为理念的最引人注目的研究者。

津巴多以前的一位学生、临床心理学家齐诺·弗兰科 *，曾经和津巴多一起研究了英雄行为的话题，他现在是津巴多的英雄创想计划项目的一名顾问。他在 2006 年的一篇文章中写道，怀揣"英雄创想"[5]可以在早期就预测和决定英雄行为，他把英雄行为定义为"想象面临身体危险和社会危险情境的能力，和这些情境产生的假想问题作斗争的能力，考虑自己的行为和结果的能力"。[6] 本质上，在这些问题发生之前去透彻地思考它们的可能性，就可以在问题发生时更好地做准备。

与此同时，社会心理学家克雷格·哈尼可能会继续研究监狱政策并倡导监狱改革。许多在监狱方面进行研究的社会学家承认美国政策制定者在很大程度上都忽视了他们的工作。然而，哈尼还是保持乐观态度，他认为，他的研究以及从监狱研究和社会心理学获得的更广泛证据最终将影响美国公众和政界对监狱在社会中的作用的看法。他在 2005 年出版的一本书中写道，美国大规模监禁 * 的政策成本"已经开始在全国许多社区以显著而令人不安的方式显现出来，并急剧上升……越来越多的人认为，是时候认真反思我们的所作所为了。"[7] 哈尼和其他监狱政策研究者特别希望找到一种刑事司法途径，能够更有效地改造罪犯，避免当前美国监狱造成的心理伤害，并且大大降低当前大规模监禁所需要的资金成本。

小结

《路西法效应》为最著名的心理学研究之一——斯坦福监狱实验——提供了一份最具可读性且内容最全面的报告。仅这一点就使它成为学生的宝贵读物。但这本书远不止此，它对许多强大的社会和群体压力加以详细分析，比如从众和去个性化，这些对理解津巴多在情境力量方面的立场都是不可或缺的。即使读者对这种力量持怀疑态度，津巴多在书中呈现的现象对了解社会心理学领域也是至关重要的。并且，因为这些力量可能会以大多数人觉得反感的方式影响行为，因此人们会觉得这本书很有启发意义。这本书对一些悲剧事件，比如许多读者可能觉得难以理解的阿布格莱布监狱虐囚事件，提出了深刻的见解。

美国社会心理学家罗伯特·莱文表示："这本书很重要，不仅应当成为社会学家的必读书目，而且政治家、决策者、教育者乃至任何受到自我毁灭力量困扰的人都应该读一读，而美国和世界其他国家似乎正走向自我毁灭。"[8] 莱文和津巴多一样，都希望对情境因素的了解能让人们更少地受到它们带来的负面影响。

然而，津巴多最后也传递了乐观的思想，并号召广大读者行动起来："我们每一个人都可能做坏事。但是，我们每个人的内心也同样住着一位英雄；如果内心的英雄能被唤醒，那么他就有可能为他人做出巨大的贡献。"[9]

---

1. 乔治·R.马斯特罗扬尼："津巴多的苹果"，《社会问题和公共政策分析》第 7 卷，2007 年第 1 期，第 251 页。

2. 马斯特罗扬尼："津巴多的苹果"，第 251 页。

3. "英雄创想计划是什么？"英雄创想计划，登录日期 2015 年 9 月 27 日，http://heroicimagination.org/。

4. 菲利普·津巴多："什么造就了英雄？"，《至善科学中心》，2011 年 1 月 18 日，登录日期 2015 年 9 月 27 日，http://greatergood.berkeley.edu/article/item/what_makes_a_hero/。

5. 齐诺·弗兰科和菲利普·津巴多："平庸之壮举"，《至善科学中心》，2006 年 9 月 1 日，登录日期 2015 年 9 月 27 日，http://greatergood.berkeley.edu/article/item/the_banality_of_heroism。

6. 弗兰科和津巴多："平庸之壮举"。

7. 克雷格·哈尼：《改革刑罚：监禁之痛的心理极限》，华盛顿：美国心理学会，

2006 年，第 x 页。

8. 罗伯特·莱文："人犯下的罪行"，《美国科学家》，2007 年 9—10 月，登录日期 2015 年 9 月 15 日，http://americanscientist.org/bookshelf/content2/2007/5/the-evil-that-men-do。

9. 津巴多："什么造就了英雄？"

术语表

1. **阿布格莱布**：巴格达的一座监狱，在 2003 年美国领导的伊拉克战争期间用以关押伊拉克囚犯和被拘留者。因美国士兵对那里的囚犯实施生理、心理和性虐待被曝光，虐囚丑闻随之爆发。

2. **美国心理学会（APA）**：代表美国心理学家的科学和专业组织，是美国最大的专业心理学研究机构。

3. **大赦国际**：一个成立于 20 世纪 60 年代的非政府性组织，起初旨在保护政治犯的人权，如今在人权领域起着更广泛的作用。

4. **心理科学协会（APS）**：一个国际非营利性组织（前称美国心理协会），关注心理学领域研究的道德规范、公众兴趣以及宣传推广。

5. **威权主义的**：一种人格特质，既对权威高度服从，又支持对下属的压迫。

6. **平庸之恶**：这个术语由作家汉娜·阿伦特提出，用以描述纳粹战犯阿道夫·艾希曼的罪行。艾希曼声称他在二战中负责屠杀犹太人只是"履行自己的职责"。这个术语后来用以指代一种观点，即邪恶是普遍存在的，普通人也可能作恶。

7. **BBC 监狱研究**：社会心理学家史蒂芬·赖歇尔和 S. 亚历山大·哈斯拉姆开展的一项实证研究，目的在于和斯坦福监狱实验进行对比研究。这项研究于 2002 年在英国广播公司以电视纪录片的形式播出。

8. **行为主义**：一种重要的学习理论，在整个 20 世纪，特别是 20 世纪中期在心理学界非常盛行。支持该理论的学者往往认为应该研究行为而非认知因素（也就是思维），所以他们倾向于研究可观察的行为。

9. **英国广播公司（BBC）**：英国一家提供电视和媒体服务的广播公司。

10. **天主教神职人员性侵案**：主要发生在 20 世纪末和 21 世纪初的一系

列天主教会神职人员性侵儿童事件，他们受到指控并判罪。

11. **认知**：与知识相关的所有心智能力和心智过程，包括记忆、注意力、解决问题、学习等。

12. **认知革命**：始于 20 世纪 50 年代，发生在心理学、人类学和语言学等多个领域的广泛运动。这场运动聚焦于研究人类用来理解世界并与世界互动的内在思想、态度、动机和价值观。

13. **从众**：由于群体的规范和其他社会压力，个人通常使其自身的认知和行为与群体的认知和行为保持一致。

14. **军事法庭**：主要审理军人案件并作出判决的法庭。

15. **询问情况**：涉及到人类受试者的研究中具有的一种实验后干预过程，向参与者提供有关研究的更多信息，并调查他们因为参与研究而产生的心理压力。

16. **去人性化**：忽视或贬低他人的人类属性，通常将他们视为没有感情、低人一等，就像动物一样。

17. **去个性化**：在社会心理学中指的是，个体由于融入群体或处于匿名状态而丧失其自我意识和许多倾向。

18. **需求特性**：在实验研究中，参与者发现了研究的目的，进而影响他们的态度或行为。

19. **性情**：心理学术语，指个体的内在性格，如人格特质。

20. **平等主义**：一种倡导平等对待所有人的社会学说。

21. **安然造假丑闻**：2001 年，美国能源巨头安然公司陷入大范围的公司腐败和会计造假，事件导致公司破产，一些高层锒铛入狱。

22. **贫民区**：城市中被隔离的贫穷地区，居住着少数族裔，他们一般没有其他住所。

23. **大萧条**：美国历史上最严重的一场经济衰退，始于 1929 年，并一直持续到 20 世纪 30 年代末。

24. **英雄创想计划**：菲利普·津巴多创立的一个非营利性组织，旨在研究、讲授和鼓励英雄行为。

25. **人类受试者研究审查委员会 / 机构审查委员会**：专门审查、监督和批准由人参与实验研究的组织。在 20 世纪早期到中期，许多研究用欺骗的手段或其他现在认为不道德的方式对待受试者，在这一背景下，这些组织应运而生。

26. **个人主义**：一种思维模式，人们认为自己是个体，而不是群体中的一员。

27. **互动主义**：社会心理学和人格心理学领域的一种普遍的观点，认为行为在很大程度上是由性情因素和情境因素相互作用决定的。

28. **伊拉克战争**：美国在 2003 年领导的一场旷日持久的入侵伊拉克的战争。

29. **路西法**：基督教传统中的一个堕落天使，后来成为邪恶的象征。

30. **大规模监禁**：相对较高比例的人口被囚禁。

31. **归属感**：心理学术语，指的是人们希望被群体和社会圈子所接纳、成为其中一员的基本需求。

32. **规范**：心理学术语，指的是在任何一个特定的群体中（无论是小群体还是更大的群体或人群）为大家接受的标准、价值观和符合预期的行为和思维方式。每个群体定义自己的规范，某一群体制定的规范未必为其他群体所接受。

33. **服从权威**：对权威的屈从或顺服。心理学家斯坦利·米尔格拉姆开展的研究表明服从权威对许多人的行为有着惊人的影响。

34. **服从权威研究**：斯坦利·米尔格拉姆于 20 世纪 60 年代早期在耶鲁大学开展的一项研究。他指示志愿者对陌生人实施电击，并声称这是一项关于学习行为的实验。大多数参与者并不知道这不是真的电击，尽管他们心里感到害怕和痛苦，但还是实施了强度越来越大的电击。这项有争议的实验揭示了权威人物对人们行为的影响力量。

35. **同辈压力**：一个群体的社会影响力，它会促使同龄人和其他群体成员的态度和行为发生转变。

36. **人格心理学**：心理学的一个领域，关注人们在有意义的心理变量上的差异。

37. **人格—情境之争**：人格心理学历史上的一场持久争论，焦点是人格 / 性情因素还是情境因素影响行为。

38. **政治学家**：对人类政治行为和结构（如政府机构、政治选择的方式以及国际关系等）进行系统研究的人。

39. **积极心理学**：心理学的分支，关注发展成就，而不是异常行为的治疗。

40. **情境力量**：情境可能会对人类行为产生强烈影响的观点。

41. **"强盗山洞"实验**：由社会心理学家穆扎弗·谢里夫于 1954 年进行的一项心理学实验。他将在俄克拉荷马州开展夏令营活动的小男孩们随机分成两组，他们互相争夺营地资源，结果导致偏见、敌意，最后爆发群体之间的冲突。

42. **卢旺达种族大屠杀**：卢旺达占人口多数的胡图族于 1994 年发动了一场大屠杀，多达 100 万人被害，其中绝大多数是占人口少数的图西族。

43. **施虐狂**：故意施暴或以虐待他人为乐。

44. **施莱辛格报告**：由詹姆斯·施莱辛格于 2004 年领导的对阿布格莱布监狱虐囚事件的独立调查报告。

45. **情境**：外部世界的某些方面，是分析邪恶产生的重点。情境可以指周围环境的任何方面，包括他人、天气、外部的规则和法律等。

46. **情境决定论者**：指的是通常相信情境力量能够在很大程度上决定处于那些情境中的个体的行为的人，他们通常更愿意从情境而不是从人格特质的角度来解释行为。

47. **情境压力**：一个人周围的情境施加在他 / 她身上的强大心理压力，无论他 / 她是否意识到这些压力。

48. **社会学家**：研究人类社会的历史、本质、形成和结构的学者。

49. **社会心理学**：心理学的一个领域，关注情境如何影响人们的思想、情感和行为。

50. **单独监禁**：一种监禁方式，将犯人单独关押在牢房中，不允许和其他人，甚至是和其他犯人有任何接触。

51. **斯坦福监狱实验**：菲利普·津巴多于 1971 年在斯坦福大学进行的一项心理学研究。在临时监狱中，12 位志愿者被随机分成两组，分别充当狱卒或囚犯。实验原计划持续两周，但由于狱卒虐待受其控制的囚犯，不得不提前终止。

52. **系统性因素**：大规模组织或系统（如政府、文化和经济）造成的影响。

53. **特质**：人格心理学术语，指的是性情或在某种程度上一致的行为或认知模式。

54. **美国国防部**：美国政府的一个部门，负责美国国家安全和武装力量。

55. **越南战争**：发生在 1955—1975 年间越共支持的北越和 1961 年以后美国军队支持的南越之间的武装冲突。战争各方（包括美军）都犯下了暴行。

56. **第二次世界大战**：发生在 1939—1945 年间的一场全球规模的战争，战争双方是轴心国（德国、意大利和日本）和同盟国（英国、苏联、美国等）。

人名表

1. 所罗门·阿希（1907—1996），波兰社会心理学家，宾夕法尼亚大学荣退教授，以研究从众行为而闻名。

2. 阿里·巴努阿齐齐，伊朗裔美国政治学家，波士顿学院教授，以研究中东政治文化而闻名。

3. 小卢迪·T.本杰明（1945年生），美国心理学家，得克萨斯农工大学教授。他的著作记录了心理学向科学的转变。

4. 乔治·W.布什（1946年生），美国第43任总统，共和党人，2001—2009年间执政。

5. 托马斯·卡纳汉，美国组织心理学家，曾任孟菲斯大学教授。他因重新审视斯坦福监狱实验而闻名。

6. 迪克·切尼（1941年生），美国第46任副总统。共和党人，2001—2009年期间担任美国总统乔治·W.布什的副手。

7. 苏珊·T.菲斯克（1952年生），美国社会心理学家，普林斯顿大学教授，主要研究社会认知、偏见和刻板印象等。

8. 齐诺·弗兰科，美国威斯康星医学院临床心理学教授。他的著作研究并定义了英雄行为。

9. 伊万·弗里德里克（1966年生），美军前中士。2004年，他因前一年在伊拉克的阿布格莱布监狱虐待被拘禁者而被指控犯有战争罪。在承认包括同谋、虐待被拘禁者、殴打和猥亵行为等多项指控后，他被判处八年监禁，开除军籍，永不录用。

10. 克雷格·哈尼，美国社会心理学家，加利福尼亚大学圣克鲁兹分校教授，因研究监禁造成的心理影响和监狱的有效性而闻名。

11. S.亚历山大·哈斯拉姆（1962年生），澳大利亚社会心理学家，昆士兰大学教授。他的著作探讨了从众行为和专制统治，并对斯坦

福监狱实验和斯坦利·米尔格拉姆的权威服从研究的阐释提出了质疑。

12. **罗伯特·莱文**，美国社会心理学家，加利福尼亚州立大学弗雷斯诺分校教授，以研究不同文化背景的人如何利用和感知时间而著称。

13. **乔治·R.马斯特罗扬尼**，美国心理学家，美国空军学院教授。他的著作将心理学研究应用于军事训练和实践。

14. **罗丝·麦克德莫特**，美国政治学家，布朗大学国际关系学教授，因研究政治行为的预测因素而闻名。

15. **山姆·麦克法兰**，美国社会心理学家，西肯塔基大学荣退教授，主要研究人权问题。

16. **斯坦利·米尔格拉姆**（1933—1984），美国社会心理学家，耶鲁大学教授。他著名的权威服从研究揭示了人们对权威力量的服从程度。

17. **沃尔特·米歇尔**（1930年生），美国心理学家，哥伦比亚大学教授，研究自我控制，并从互动主义的视角研究人格。

18. **赛玛卡·穆瓦赫迪**，伊朗裔美国社会学家，马萨诸塞大学社会学教授，其研究涵盖社会结构和精神病理学之间的关系。

19. **史蒂芬·赖歇尔**，英国社会心理学家，圣安德鲁斯大学教授，研究群体中的人类行为，并从事领导者和暴政方面的研究。

20. **唐纳德·拉姆斯菲尔德**（1932年生），1975—1977年间任美国第13任国防部长；2001—2006年期间任美国第21任国防部长。

21. **卡罗琳·谢里夫**（1922—1982），美国社会心理学家，大部分职业生涯在宾夕法尼亚州立大学度过，研究群体冲突和合作。

22. **穆扎弗·谢里夫**（1906—1988），土耳其裔美国社会心理学家。他的重要著作研究了社会规范和由争夺资源引起的社会冲突，他设计了"强盗山洞"实验。

23. 琼·E.西贝尔，美国心理学家，加利福尼亚州立大学荣退教授，以从事科学和实验伦理方面的研究而闻名。

24. 杰弗里·A.辛普森，美国社会心理学家，明尼苏达大学教授，以研究人与人之间的亲密关系而闻名。

25. 马丁·B.托里奇，新西兰社会学家，新西兰奥塔哥大学教授。他的著作涵盖实验伦理研究。

WAYS IN TO THE TEXT

- Born in 1933, Philip Zimbardo is an American social psychologist* and professor emeritus at Stanford University. Social psychology is the study of how people's social surroundings influence their thought processes, memories, learning, and behavior. He is known for his groundbreaking work on the effect that certain circumstances have on behavior.

- In *The Lucifer Effect* (2007), Zimbardo details the power of situations* (that is, aspects of a context that are external to the person serving as a focal point of analysis) to create evil. Evil here can refer to actions and people who intentionally cause physical, psychological, financial, or emotional harm and pain to others.

- Zimbardo uses his insights to detail in the book how and why some situations cause people to conform* to an idea of evil. Conforming is when individuals match their thought processes and behaviors to that of a wider group because of powerful social pressures.

Who Is Philip Zimbardo?

Philip Zimbardo, author of *The Lucifer Effect: Understanding How Good People Turn Evil* (2007), was born in 1933 in the South Bronx of New York City, an area he would later describe as "a ghetto"* (a slum, usually occupied by a single minority community). Much of his childhood overlapped with the Great Depression* of 1929 to the late 1930s—an extreme economic recession causing profound financial hardship to much of the population of the United States. Zimbardo grew up poor.

In *The Lucifer Effect* (2007), Zimbardo describes how these circumstances affected his thinking and eventually his career, writing: "Urban ghetto life is all about surviving by developing useful 'street-smart' strategies. That means figuring out who has power that can be used against you or to help you, whom to avoid, and with whom you should ingratiate yourself."[1] Zimbardo explains that these experiences made him aware of the key roles held by power, and by particular situations, in affecting behavior and life outcomes.

His upbringing provoked his interest in psychology. In 1959, Zimbardo completed his PhD in psychology at Yale University, joining the psychology faculty at Stanford University in California in 1968, where he has remained ever since. Now professor emeritus at Stanford, Zimbardo remains active in both research and political activism.

In 2012, he wrote that since conducting a key piece of research, his "Stanford Prison Experiment"* of 1971, he had "become a prison activist."[2] He has often advised and lectured policymakers and the judiciary on the negative psychological consequences of prison on prisoners. He is also founder of the Heroic Imagination Project (HIP),* a research body "dedicated to promoting heroism in everyday life."

Besides the Great Depression, two other major sociopolitical events shaped Zimbardo and his research. In the 1950s, many social psychologists began to study the topics of power, obedience, and evil in an attempt to explain the events and horrors that had occurred during World War II,* the global war of 1939–45 that began with Germany's invasion of Poland and ultimately involved many of the world's nations. This was also of interest to Zimbardo.

Later, he opposed the United States' military involvement in the Vietnam War,* the 1955–75 armed conflict between communist North Vietnam and South Vietnam, whose forces were supported by the US military after 1961.This opposition triggered his political and social activism.

What Does *The Lucifer Effect* Say?

In *The Lucifer Effect*, Zimbardo aims to provide psychological explanations of instances of evil.

Though he chooses not to explicitly define evil in the text, he relies on specific historical examples of "violence, anonymity, aggression, vandalism, torture, and terrorism"[3] to provide an implicit framework for what he considers to be evil. He specifically concentrates on the prison abuses perpetrated by members of the US military at Abu Ghraib prison* in Iraq, during the American-led invasion of that country in 2003.

In this case, American Army personnel tasked with guarding Iraqi detainees at Abu Ghraib prison repeatedly committed serious physical, psychological, and sexual abuse on the captives, often taking photographs to record the abuse. To many observers this was a surprising instance of sadistic* behavior (a sadist is a person who gets enjoyment from being violent or cruel, or causing pain to others). Zimbardo, however, claims that the abuse at Abu Ghraib should not be so surprising, as his 1971 Stanford Prison Experiment (SPE) demonstrated that ordinary people—even those who genuinely believed they would be incapable of harming others—are indeed capable of what Zimbardo calls "evil."

Zimbardo's core message in *The Lucifer Effect* is that situations can exert a great power over us. To illustrate this, he offers a detailed retelling and analysis of the SPE, a psychology study he designed and ran at Stanford University. The 24 participants were volunteers who agreed to live or work in a makeshift prison for two weeks. Zimbardo and his research assistants randomly assigned them to the role of either a prisoner or a guard, while he served as the prison superintendent. Under instruction to maintain order, the guards quickly began to abuse their roles, with Zimbardo observing as they psychologically and physically abused the prisoners. After just six days, the experiment had to be halted.

In *The Lucifer Effect*, published 26 years later, Zimbardo writes that the power of the overall situation and a host of situational factors were responsible for the transformation of the guards. He states that the SPE "emerged as a powerful illustration of the potentially toxic impact of bad systems and bad situations in making good people behave in pathological ways that are alien to their nature."[4]

In the book, Zimbardo uses his detailed findings from the SPE, along with other supporting studies accumulated since, to analyze other instances of sadistic, shocking, and evil events that have occurred throughout history, focusing on the prison abuses at Abu Ghraib.

Zimbardo becomes part of the story, just as he was in the SPE. He served as expert witness in the trial of one of the guards, Ivan Frederick,* who was eventually convicted of the assault and maltreatment of detainees at Abu Ghraib. The social psychologist

Robert Levine* wrote in his review of the book: "By the time Zimbardo has finished describing Frederick's transformation from idealistic soldier to abuser, Abu Ghraib feels eerily indistinguishable from the Stanford Prison Experiment. It is as if the Iraqi prison had been designed by twisted social psychologists who wanted to replicate Zimbardo's experiment using real guards and prisoners."[5]

Finally, Zimbardo discusses how systemic factors* (that is, the influence of large-scale systems such as governments, cultures, economies, and organizations) tend to set up the bad conditions that allow for the bad situations that, in turn, elicit evil behavior. He concludes the text with a study on how people can avoid these bad situations and resist situational forces* to behave badly, much as he claims someone acting heroically would. Such situational forces are psychological pressures that are placed on a person by the circumstances surrounding them, whether they are aware of these pressures or not.

Why Does *The Lucifer Effect* Matter?

While *The Lucifer Effect* includes a wealth of information on social psychology, research ethics, and many historical events, it is mainly important because of its in-depth investigation of Zimbardo's own Stanford Prison Experiment—now recognized as a seminal study in the field of psychology. In examining the experiment, Zimbardo describes the social and psychological factors he believes are largely responsible for the outcome of the SPE (along with other evils such as the abuse at Abu Ghraib prison). He also analyses the Enron* scandal (an instance of widespread institutional corruption and fraud discovered at the US energy company Enron Corporation in 2001), the Rwanda genocides* (where up to one million people, mostly from the Tutsi ethnic minority, were slaughtered in 1994, primarily by Rwanda's Hutu majority), and the Roman Catholic Church sexual-abuse scandals* (the multiple cases of sexual abuse committed by Catholic clergymen worldwide in recent decades).

Yet Zimbardo offers hope and advice for readers of *The Lucifer Effect* so they can better understand instances of "evil" behavior: "I have proposed that we give greater consideration and more weight to situational and systemic processes than we typically do when we are trying to account for aberrant behaviors and seeming personality changes. Human behavior is always subject to situational forces."[6]

Most of all, Zimbardo hopes that a better knowledge of these treacherous situational forces allow people, in their own lives, to detect and resist the powerful pressure to act badly in certain situations:"In all the research cited and in our real-world examples, there were always some individuals who resisted [situational influences and evil] , who did not yield to temptation. What delivered them from evil was not some inherent magical goodness but rather, more likely, an understanding, however intuitive, of mental and social tactics of resistance."[7]

For Zimbardo, heroism, like evil, is not something people are born with, but something his readers, and anyone, can learn to develop.

Finally, *The Lucifer Effect* offers Zimbardo's insights into some of the controversies stimulated by the Stanford Prison Experiment and also his wider ideas. Referencing those controversies throughout the book, Zimbardo provides both analytical and historical background into one of the key criticisms of the experiment: that it was an unethical study. Zimbardo dedicates a chapter specifically to research ethics and the SPE, discussing his beliefs on the experiment's ethics and his own ethical failings.

---

1. Philip Zimbardo, *The Lucifer Effect: Understanding How Good People Turn Evil* (New York: Random House, 2007), xi.

2. Scott Drury, Scott A. Hutchens, Duane E. Shuttlesworth, and Carole L. White, "Philip G. Zimbardo on His Career and the Stanford Prison Experiment's 40th Anniversary," *History of Psychology* 15, no. 2 (2012): 162.

3. Zimbardo, *Lucifer*, xi.

4. Zimbardo, *Lucifer*, 195.

5. Robert Levine, "The Evil That Men Do," *American Scientist*, September-October 2007, accessed September 15, 2015, http://www. americanscientist.org/bookshelf/content2/2007/5/the-evil-that-men-do.

6. Zimbardo, *Lucifer*, 445.

7. Zimbardo, *Lucifer*, xiii.

SECTION 1
INFLUENCES

THE AUTHOR AND THE HISTORICAL CONTEXT

KEY POINTS

- *The Lucifer Effect* is the most extensive analysis of Philip Zimbardo's famed 1971 Stanford Prison Experiment (SPE).* This study had gained renewed significance as Zimbardo has applied his findings from the SPE to offer insights into more recent—and real—acts of evil.

- As a student, Zimbardo worked in New York City's theater district. He developed an appreciation for, and understanding of, drama and production values (the details and finesse that contribute to a successful theatrical experience) that were later apparent in his design of the SPE.

- Several historical events pushed Zimbardo toward a career in social psychology* (the study of how thought and behavior are influenced by social surroundings) and political and social activism. They were, in particular, the Great Depression,* an economic downturn that began in 1929, and the Vietnam War,* a conflict in which the United States fought between 1961–75 with the loss of many lives.

Why Read This Text?

Philip Zimbardo's *The Lucifer Effect: Understanding How Good People Turn Evil* (2007) provides an account of some of the situational* factors (that is, the external factors such as context, surroundings, and so on, that affect the person being studied) that lead ordinary people to commit unethical, deviant, destructive, and "evil" behavior. In a review of *The Lucifer Effect*, the political scientist Rose McDermott* wrote, "This remarkable and riveting new book by the creator of the classic Stanford Prison Experiment (SPE) deserves to be required reading for all those interested in the intersection of psychological processes and political reality."[1]

Zimbardo draws the majority of the text's empirical evidence (that is, its evidence verifiable by observation) from his famed SPE study, conducted in 1971. That study showed how quickly ordinary people could behave in "evil" ways when placed in particular circumstances. It remains one of the most well-known, dramatic, and important experiments in social psychology.* As the social psychologist Robert Levine* writes: "The Stanford Prison Experiment has become a cornerstone of social psychology... What happened at Stanford makes it clear that insane situations can create insane behavior even in normal people."[2]

The SPE has also become one of the most reviewed and analyzed studies in the field. Yet in *The Lucifer Effect*, Zimbardo gives new life to the already seminal SPE study. He combines original and new interpretations of the experiment and introduces more recent research, as he offers explanations for many evils that have occurred in the world since the 1970s. Zimbardo provides the most extensive written account of the experiment to date— including a dramatic retelling of the entire procedure, transcripts of the study, and interviews with participants.

Zimbardo also introduces in the book a new understanding of the SPE. He explains that he has come to view systemic factors* (that is, the influence of large-scale organizations or systems) as responsible for many of the situations that elicit evil. Therefore, he sees systemic factors as worthy of examination by psychologists.

> "I guess you could say I was an intuitive psychologist and 'situationist'* from the beginning. I was born at home, hands first, in New York City's South Bronx ghetto during the Great Depression, and we moved 31 times while I was a child."
>
> —— Philip Zimbardo, *On 50 Years of Giving Psychology Away: An Interview With Philip Zimbardo*

Author's Life

Zimbardo was born in 1933 in the urban ghettos—deprived neighborhoods—of New York City, growing up poor in the years of the Great Depression. As a child he endured a lengthy hospitalization for respiratory illness, and while he was treated in isolation, he saw many sick children die around him. Zimbardo later recalled that the "experience of extreme isolation at a very formative time in my childhood really gave me a push in the direction of not only being a social psychologist, but of wanting to study things and do things that improve the quality of human life."[3]

His childhood experiences of urban poverty, and of ingratiating himself with the neighborhood gangs, were also influential. Zimbardo recalled that he and his friends "had initiation rituals that each new kid had to go through to gain admission to the gang, a series of daring deeds that had to be accomplished in one day."[4] The psychology behind such initiations became a theme of his later work, including the SPE. Zimbardo wanted to examine the willingness of ordinary people to forego their own moral standards and normal behavior simply to gain acceptance into a group.

As a teenage student, Zimbardo worked at a theater in New York's Broadway District. He later recalled that this "taught me about the virtues of performing really well"[5]—virtues that became apparent later in his elaborate production and staging of the SPE.

Zimbardo went on to complete his PhD in psychology at Yale University in 1959. In 1968, he became professor of psychology at Stanford University. Now professor emeritus at the university, Zimbardo continues to research new fields, including shyness, heroism, terrorism, and the perception of time. He is founder of the Heroic Imagination Project (HIP),* a research body dedicated to promoting heroic behavior in everyday life.

Author's Background

By his own admission, Zimbardo was shaped by three major sociopolitical events that occurred during his childhood and early career—the Great Depression, World War II,* and the Vietnam War. Foremost, Zimbardo grew up poor, like many others in America during the Great Depression. He later recalled the pain of feeling judged, and even perceived as less than human, due to his family's financial plight. In one interview, Zimbardo said that "being hurt personally triggered a curiosity about how such beliefs are formed, how attitudes can influence people's behavior, how people can feel so strongly about something they know nothing about."[6]

America's military involvement in Vietnam in the 1960s and

1970s, also influenced Zimbardo; he describes it as the trigger for his later political and social activism. A prominent anti-war campaigner, he has also demanded changes to the American prison system. In a 2012 interview, Zimbardo said, "I have too much to say, and I now have a reputation that I can use for certain causes like being against war, being a peace activist, and now, trying to create everyday heroes."[7]

1. Rose McDermott, "Reviewed Work: *The Lucifer Effect: Understanding How Good People Turn Evil* by Philip Zimbardo," *Political Psychology* 28, No. 5 (2007): 644.

2. Robert Levine, "The Evil That Men Do," *American Scientist*, September-October 2007, accessed September 15, 2015, http://www. americanscientist.org/bookshelf/content2/2007/5/the-evil-that-men-do.

3. Christina Maslach, "Emperor of the Edge," *Psychology Today*, September 1, 2000, accessed September 15, 2015, https://www.psychologytoday.com/articles/200009/emperor-the-edge.

4. Philip Zimbardo, "Recollections of a Social Psychologist's Career: An Interview with Dr. Philip Zimbardo," *Journal of Social Behavior and Personality* 14, No. 1 (1999): 2.

5. George M. Slavich, "On 50 Years of Giving Psychology Away: An Interview with Philip Zimbardo," *Teaching of Psychology* 36, no. 4 (2009): 280.

6. Maslach, "Emperor of the Edge," *Psychology Today*.

7. Scott Drury, Scott A. Hutchens, Duane E. Shuttlesworth, and Carole L. White, "Philip G. Zimbardo on His Career and the Stanford Prison Experiment's 40th Anniversary," *History of Psychology* 15, no. 2 (2012): 164.

MODULE 2
ACADEMIC CONTEXT

KEY POINTS

* In the 1960s and 1970s, there was an ongoing debate between social psychologists* (those who study how people's mental processes and behaviors are influenced by their social surroundings) and personality psychologists* (those who study individual differences in people's mental processes and behaviors). Each group argued for the relative influence of situational factors versus personality factors on a person's behavior.

* Social psychologists Muzafer Sherif* and Solomon Asch* have provided some of the strongest evidence of the power of situations* to determine behavior.

* Yale University psychology professor Stanley Milgram,* whose work particularly influenced Philip Zimbardo, provided even more dramatic evidence of the power of situations.

The Work in Its Context

Although Philip Zimbardo's *The Lucifer Effect: Understanding How Good People Turn Evil* was published in 2007, it is largely a retelling of the 1971 Stanford Prison Experiment (SPE).* As a result, the book is a product of two eras.

In the early 1970s, psychology was in the midst of what people called the cognitive revolution.* This began in the 1950s and affected a number of academic fields including psychology, anthropology, and linguistics.

The cognitive revolution was broadly a move away from

behaviorism,* which concentrated on studying observable behaviors, replacing it with a focus on the study of a person's cognitions*—that is, the inner workings of the mind, thoughts, attitudes, motivations, mental abilities, memories, and values that make up a person's inner life.

Zimbardo's specific field was social psychology (the study of how people's social surroundings influence their cognitions and behaviors). Social psychology and its partner field, personality psychology* (the study of individual differences in people's thought processes and behaviors), were also in debate over the primary influence of behavior. Was it the person and his or her internal attitudes—what psychologists call dispositions*—that determined behavior? Or did the power of situations outweigh individual personalities?

Walter Mischel,* professor of psychology at Columbia University, is often credited as sparking this so-called "person-situation debate."* Mischel described the debate as being about the consistency "with which the same person reacts to situations that ostensibly are relatively similar (that is, selected to evoke the same trait*), and most important, the utility of predictions based on global trait inferences."[1] In the field of personality psychology, a "trait" refers to a disposition, or a somewhat consistent pattern of behavior or cognition. Mischel questioned whether these traits can reliably and meaningfully predict behavior.

Mischel argued the importance of considering dispositions, situations, *and* the interaction between them—an approach described as "interactionist."* However, other psychologists focused their research on just one factor. At that time, Zimbardo concentrated on situations as the prime determinant of behavior.

By the time *The Lucifer Effect* was published in 2007, most psychologists had accepted that dispositional factors (internal characteristics such as personality traits) and situational factors (the conscious or unconscious psychological pressures placed on a person by the situation around them), and their interactions were all integral for predicting and explaining behavior. A more recent research movement, named positive psychology,* had also become relevant by that time. Proponents of positive psychology seek to change the questions that psychologists traditionally ask—away from a focus on negative outcomes, such as how and why people become depressed, and towards a focus on positive outcomes, such as how and why people thrive.

> *"Beginning in the 1950s, attention in social psychology started to turn toward the powerful and sometimes counterintuitive effects that social situations could have on how people think, feel, and behave."*
>
> —— Ludy T. Benjamin Jr.* and Jeffry A. Simpson,*
> *The Power of the Situation*

Overview of the Field

By the mid-1950s, a number of social psychologists were already successfully proving the power with which situational factors can determine human behavior. An early and clear example was the 1954 Robber's Cave Experiment* conducted by the social psychologists Muzafer Sherif* and Carolyn Sherif.* At a summer camp in Oklahoma in the United States, they randomly divided 22 young boys into two groups and then placed them in a series of manipulated situations. As a result, the boys' attitudes and behaviors changed. After competitive games, hostility and stereotyping increased between groups. Meanwhile, after cooperative tasks, hostility and stereotyping decreased.

Around the same time, the social psychologist Solomon Asch ran a series of studies on conformity* (when individuals match their thoughts and behaviors to that of a wider group, due to social pressures) that highlighted the power of situations to dictate behavior, often in unexpected ways. In his most well-known task, he presented study participants with a straight black line and then asked them to choose which one matched the original from a set of straight black lines of varying lengths. Unbeknownst to the participant, he or she was not surrounded by fellow participants. Rather, Asch had paid everyone else in the group and instructed them to give a (matching) incorrect response purposely.

This study clearly illustrated the power of the situation and of a majority group. Although it was obvious which of the lines did match in length, participants often publicly submitted the incorrect answer, conforming to the answer that the majority of the group provided. Asch reported: "A substantial proportion of subjects yielded once their confidence was shaken. The presumed rightness of the majority deprived them of the resolution to report their own observations."[2] The Sherif and Asch studies demonstrate how situational pressures, such as the formation of groups and a person's subsequent conformity to that group, can cause people to behave unexpectedly.

Academic Influences

In his work on the Stanford Prison Experiment, and on the causes of evil and heroism, Zimbardo was following in the footsteps of Sherif and Asch as he argued that situations and group pressures have enormous influence. However, the psychologist Stanley Milgram, who was also Zimbardo's friend and former high school classmate, was the person who most directly influenced him. Zimbardo later recalled that even in high school, Milgram had been fascinated by the power of situations: "Milgram was concerned about the Holocaust even back then... His work on blind obedience to authority really derived from his concern about whether the same thing could happen here [in the US]."[3] "The Holocaust" refers to the genocide, orchestrated by Nazi Germany and its leader Adolf Hitler, of about six million European Jews and other ethnic and social minorities during World War II.*

In the early 1960s, Milgram, then psychology professor at Yale University, ran a groundbreaking "obedience to authority"* study. He instructed volunteers to give electric shocks to a stranger, allegedly for an experiment on learning. Unaware that the shocks were not real, most participants administered increasingly powerful and seemingly painful and dangerous shocks, despite their own fear and distress at doing so, simply because an experimenter instructed them to continue. Many people progressed to a level that would have been lethal if real.

Milgram's colleagues and the public were surprised by the results of the highly controversial study, which was the most dramatic illustration at the time of the power of the situation (and people's innate obedience to authorities) on behaviors. Zimbardo later argued that "[Milgram] was really the first person to say that it's not enough to think or say that you won't do something. Indeed, it's not even enough to imagine you're in a situation, because it's something about being in powerful social settings that is transformative."[4]

1. Walter Mischel, "Toward a Cognitive Social Learning Reconceptualization of Personality," *Psychological Review* 80, no. 4 (1973): 255.

2. Solomon E. Asch, "Studies of Independence and Conformity: I. A Minority of One Against a Unanimous Majority," *Psychological Monographs: General and Applied* 70, no. 9 (1956): 70.

3. George M. Slavich, "On 50 Years of Giving Psychology Away: An Interview with Philip Zimbardo." *Teaching of Psychology* 36, no. 4 (2009): 279.

4. Slavich, "Giving," 279.

MODULE 3
THE PROBLEM

KEY POINTS

- In 2003, during the United States' invasion of Iraq, American military personnel working at Abu Ghraib* prison in Baghdad committed physical abuse, sexual assaults, and torture on Iraqi detainees. There were also claims that American psychologists were complicit in the abuse.

- Many social psychologists* and independent investigators argued that situational factors* were largely to blame for the abuse at Abu Ghraib.

- Philip Zimbardo, referencing his Stanford Prison Experiment (SPE),* became an expert witness in the trial of one of the Abu Ghraib guards and was outspoken about the likely role of situational factors.

Core Question

Philip Zimbardo's *The Lucifer Effect: Understanding How Good People Turn Evil* (2007) seeks to examine and explain the prisoner abuses committed at Abu Ghraib prison in Baghdad in 2003. US military prison guards there carried out a sustained campaign of psychological and physical torture and sexual abuse of detainees, with many instances recorded on camera.

Zimbardo was already considered a leading expert on prison mentality and sadistic* behavior (that is, finding pleasure in causing suffering to others.) He entered the debate on Abu Ghraib in 2004, writing an opinion piece for the *Boston Globe* that stated, "Unless we learn the dynamics of 'why,' we will never be able to counteract the powerful forces that can transform ordinary people into evil perpetrators."[1] In this way, Zimbardo urged both researchers and the public to consider the importance of situational causes in the Abu Ghraib case.

Soon after the abuse at Abu Ghraib came to the public's attention, some news reports claimed that American psychologists were also involved in the administration of torture techniques on detainees captured in Iraq. Additional reports soon implicated the American Psychological Association (APA),* the scientific and professional organization that represents psychologists in the United States. These reports claimed the APA was assisting the American government in its search for effective interrogation techniques. People began to question whether such techniques amounted to torture—especially as the APA had expressly forbidden its members from supporting torture.

In 2006, the APA's committee on ethics and national security reiterated its previous stance, declaring that "there are no exceptional circumstances whatsoever... that may be invoked as a justification for torture, including the invocation of laws, regulations or orders."[2]

Nonetheless, various sources and reports continued to accuse APA members and leaders of either supporting or administering torture tactics. By drawing on his experiences from the Stanford Prison Experiment (SPE), Zimbardo was uniquely placed to address the abuses at Abu Ghraib, the American government's use of torture, and the role of psychologists in both of those contentious situations.

"The horrifying photos of young Iraqis abused by American soldiers have shocked the world with their depictions of human degradation, forcing us to acknowledge that some of our beloved soldiers have committed barbarous acts of cruelty and sadism."

——Philip Zimbardo, *Power Turns Good Soldiers into "Bad Apples"*

The Participants

Most social psychologists, when writing about the abuse at Abu Ghraib and the acceptance of torture by military officials and psychologists, tended to rely on situational explanations, arguing that the perpetrators had been affected by various psychological pressures created by the wider situations around them.

To support their accounts, these scholars often referenced the psychologist Stanley Milgram's* obedience studies (in which volunteers had been prepared to administer powerful electric shocks to strangers on the orders of an authority figure) and Philip Zimbardo's SPE (where ordinary people had rapidly become abusive of other volunteers who were under their control).

The social psychologist Susan T. Fiske* called Milgram's and Zimbardo's work "illuminating" in relation to the case of Abu Ghraib, writing: "Guards abuse prisoners in conformity* with what other guards do, in order to fulfill a potent role; this is illustrated by the Stanford Prison study."[3] Fiske argues, too, that these findings would be of benefit if considered when official policies were being formed: "Society holds individuals responsible for their actions, as the military court-martial* recognizes, but social psychology suggests we should also hold responsible peers and superiors who control the social context."[4]

In 2004, the US Department of Defense (DoD),* the branch of government charged with military matters, commissioned an independent panel to investigate the Abu Ghraib abuse case. The panel's findings also allocated blame to both situational factors and the higher authorities involved in the prison, as well as the wider US military. The committee presented its findings in the Schlesinger report,* an independent investigation into the Abu Ghraib prison abuse led by James Schlesinger in 2004, noting: "The abuses were not just the failure of some individuals to follow known standards, and they are more than the failure of a few leaders to enforce proper discipline."[5] The committee continued: "There is both institutional and personal responsibility at higher levels."[6]

The Contemporary Debate

Using both academic channels and the press, Zimbardo spoke publicly about the similarities between the events and abuses at Abu Ghraib and those that occurred during his Stanford Prison Experiment (SPE). Using his findings from the SPE, Zimbardo argued that situational and systemic factors were primarily at fault for the abuses at the Iraqi prison. In 2004, he wrote an opinion piece in the *Boston Globe*, saying that he considered the American soldiers involved in the abuse were probably "once-good apples, soured and corrupted by an evil barrel."[7] He also referred to the psychologist Stanley Milgram's obedience studies to reinforce this point.

Soon afterwards, in late 2004, Zimbardo participated in the legal defense of Ivan Frederick,* a staff sergeant in the US Army being court-martialed (prosecuted in a military court) for his role in the abuse and torture of detainees at Abu Ghraib. Acting for the defense team, Zimbardo and other psychologists and medical professionals assessed Frederick's psychological history. Zimbardo later served as an expert witness at the trial.

Writing in *The Lucifer Effect,* Zimbardo recalls his testimony and how he "outlined... some parallels between the Stanford Prison Experiment and the environment of abuse at Abu Ghraib Prison."[8] He also "argued that the situation had brought out the aberrant behaviors in which [Frederick] engaged and for which he is both sorry and guilty."[9]

Social psychologists and the military all seemed to agree that situational factors were evident in the Abu Ghraib abuses. However, Zimbardo was not convinced that the court-martial received the message, and he was displeased with Frederick's sentence, which included eight years in a military prison. Zimbardo believed the US government and military wished to adopt and promote the idea that these were a "few rogue soldiers, the 'bad apples' in the otherwise good US Army barrel."[10]

---

1. Philip G. Zimbardo, "Power turns good soldiers into 'bad apples,'" *The Boston Globe*, May 9, 2004, accessed September 16, 2015, http://www. boston.com/news/globe/editorial_opinion/oped/ articles/2004/05/09/power_turns_good_soldiers_into_bad_apples/.

2. Olivia Moorehead-Slaughter, "Ethics and National Security," *Monitor on Psychology*, April 2006, accessed September 17, 2015, http://www.apa. org/monitor/apr06/security.aspx.

3. Susan T. Fiske, L. T. Harris, and A. J. Cuddy. "Social Psychology. Why Ordinary People Torture Enemy Prisoners." *Science* 306, no. 5701 (2004): 1482-3.

4. Fiske et al., *Ordinary*, 1482.

5. John H. Cushman, Jr., "Outside Panel Faults Leaders of Pentagon for Prisoner Abuse," *New York Times*, August 24, 2004, accessed September 17, 2015, http://www.nytimes.com/2004/08/24/politics/24CND-ABUS.html.

6. Cushman, Jr., "Outside Panel Faults Leaders of Pentagon for Prisoner Abuse".

7. Zimbardo, "Power turns good soldiers into 'bad apples.'"

8. Philip Zimbardo, *The Lucifer Effect: Understanding How Good People Turn Evil* (New York: Random House, 2007), 370.

9. Zimbardo, *Lucifer*, 370.

10. Zimbardo, *Lucifer*, 371.

MODULE 4
THE AUTHOR'S CONTRIBUTION

KEY POINTS

- In *The Lucifer Effect*, Philip Zimbardo aims to illustrate the power of situations,* relying primarily on evidence from his 1971 Stanford Prison Experiment (SPE)* and the prison abuses at Abu Ghraib.*

- Zimbardo had unprecedented access to the data from both the SPE and Abu Ghraib, allowing him to make comparisons that others could not.

- Susan T. Fiske* and other social psychologists also promoted the "situationist"* school of thought, which argues that situations are often responsible for eliciting evil behaviors from ordinary people.

Author's Aims

In *The Lucifer Effect* Philip Zimbardo aims to provide both evidence and theory on when, how, and why certain situations can lead ordinary people to surprisingly sadistic* and evil behaviors. This was aimed at not only academics in his field but also the general public.

To prove his theories, Zimbardo provides an extensive account of his 1971 Stanford Prison Experiment (SPE). He then uses more recent historical examples, particularly the abuses that occurred at Abu Ghraib during the US invasion of Iraq of 2003, to support his evidence. These were particularly relatable to the SPE. Both events took place in a prison setting and, in both cases, the guards showed unexpectedly sadistic behaviors by insulting, depriving of sleep, and psychologically manipulating prisoners—although the Abu Ghraib guards also committed much more heinous acts of sexual abuse and physical torture.

In the book, Zimbardo expands his arguments beyond the situational factors that he had described and promoted in the years since the SPE. He writes of *The Lucifer Effect*, "Had I written this book shortly after the end of the Stanford Prison Experiment, I would have been content to detail the ways in which situational forces are more powerful than we think... [but] I would have missed the big picture, the bigger power for creating evil out of good—that of the System."[1]

In *The Lucifer Effect*, Zimbardo casts his attention one level up, toward the large-scale systems, such as governments, cultures, or organizations that enable the dangerous situations that, in turn, provoke and elicit evil.

Zimbardo's final major aim in the book is to examine, and share, how people can avoid the situational and systemic* factors that might push them towards bad behavior. Following early reports of the Abu Ghraib abuses, the psychologist Susan F. Fiske and her co-authors challenged the field of social psychology to better understand when and why people do *not* succumb to situational pressures. Fiske wrote in *Science* in 2004 that "explaining evils such as Abu Ghraib demonstrates scientific principles that could help to avert them."[2]

Zimbardo heeded this call, and devotes some space in *The Lucifer Effect* to providing prescriptions for how best to avoid the situational forces* that tend to elicit abusive behaviors.

"The parallels between the abuses at Abu Ghraib and the events in the SPE have given our Stanford prison experience added validity, which in turn sheds light on the psychological dynamics that contributed to creating horrific abuses in that real prison."

——Philip Zimbardo, *The Lucifer Effect: Understanding How Good People Turn Evil*

Approach

To demonstrate how powerful situations can lead ordinary people to harm others, Zimbardo relies on the data of the Stanford Prison Experiment. In *The Lucifer Effect*, he is able to provide an exhaustive account of the SPE, including detailed and previously unpublished transcripts and descriptions of video footage of the experiment.

Zimbardo was given privileged and unfettered access to information while acting as an expert witness at the court martial* (military trial) of former staff sergeant Ivan Frederick* for his actions at Abu Ghraib. Zimbardo describes in *The Lucifer Effect* how he received comprehensive access to the case. "I became more like an investigative reporter than a social psychologist,"[3] he writes. "I worked at uncovering everything I could about this young man, from intensive interviews with him and conversations and correspondence with [those who knew him]... I was given access to all of the many hundreds of digitally documented images of depravity... [and] was provided with all of the then available reports from various military and civilian investigating committees."[4]

Following these experiences, Zimbardo is able to provide an unprecedented account of how situational factors—many of which are present in most prisons—can enable some of the abuses and torture that occurred both in the SPE and at Abu Ghraib.

Those two situations were comparable due to their prison dynamic. However, Zimbardo discusses other real instances where situations have elicited evil actions in the decades since the SPE. These cases range from the corporate fraud committed at the US energy company Enron* to the 1994 genocides in Rwanda,* in which a million people from the Tutsi minority ethnic group were slaughtered, to the widespread sexual abuse committed by priests in the Roman Catholic Church.* In those varied instances, Zimbardo is able to demonstrate how many of the same situational explanations and group pressures helped to make these events possible. These include the need to belong* to social groups (social psychologists believe the desire to be accepted by others is a fundamental human need), and the pressure to conform once in a group (by altering one's thought processes and behaviors to match those shared by the wider group).

Contribution in Context

Since the 1960s, Philip Zimbardo, Stanley Milgram,* and other psychologists had been proponents of the power of the situation—the ability of situational factors to influence behavior, often overriding the influence of dispositional* factors like innate personality traits. This "situationist" school of thought was widely accepted, particularly as an explanation for the behavior of people placed in novel and stressful situations.

For many of the prison guards at Abu Ghraib, both conditions were true—they were newly stationed as prison guards and then forced to quell numerous prisoner riots, while also facing the threat of outside forces invading the prison. In 2004, Fiske and her co-authors wrote: "Virtually anyone can be aggressive if sufficiently provoked, stressed, disgruntled, or hot. The situation of the 800th Military Police Brigade guarding Abu Ghraib prisoners fit all the social conditions known to cause aggression."[5]

This school of thought was largely based on the seminal work that Milgram and Zimbardo carried out in the 1960s and 1970s. To a degree, in *The Lucifer Effect* Zimbardo is largely revisiting his own established ideology for a modern audience, as well as updating his ideas with the benefit of decades of additional evidence.

---

1. Philip Zimbardo, *The Lucifer Effect: Understanding How Good People Turn Evil* (New York: Random House, 2007), x.

2. Susan T. Fiske, L. T. Harris, and A. J. Cuddy. "Social Psychology. Why Ordinary People Torture Enemy Prisoners." *Science* 306, no. 5701 (2004): 1483.

3. Zimbardo, *Lucifer*, ix.

4. Zimbardo, *Lucifer*, ix-x.

5. Fiske, et al. "Ordinary:" 1483.

SECTION 2
IDEAS

MODULE 5
MAIN IDEAS

KEY POINTS

* In *The Lucifer Effect*, Philip Zimbardo argues that nearly everyone is capable of unethical and evil behavior when under pressure from certain situational* or systemic* factors.
* The Stanford Prison Experiment (SPE) proves the ability of seemingly normal people to act sadistically*—that is, to derive pleasure from cruel behavior—and Zimbardo suggests that similar situational and systemic factors existed at the Abu Ghraib* prison.
* In the book, Zimbardo uses metaphors to summarize his themes and provides a dramatic and detailed retelling of the SPE, which conveys the extent to which ordinary people can transform into evil.

Key Themes

In *The Lucifer Effect*, Philip Zimbardo examines the influence of external forces in "pushing us toward engaging in deviant, destructive, or evil behavior."[1] He does not define or restrict the evil behaviors that, he argues, are enabled by external forces. In fact, he does not define in the text what he considers the word "evil" to mean, despite the concept's key role. Instead, he relies on providing examples of such behaviors, concentrating on the abuses that occurred during the SPE and at Abu Ghraib prison.

Zimbardo's analysis has two key themes running through it:

• First, that good and evil are permeable (meaning, in this instance, interchangeable). Zimbardo suggests that "it is

116

possible for angels to become devils and... for devils to become angels."[2] Therefore most people are capable of both.

- Second, that external forces are more responsible than dispositional factors* (that is, an individual's own personality) for much of the world's evil. Zimbardo suggests that a hierarchy of influence exists, with systemic factors (such as governments, organizations or cultures) being the most effective conductors of evil, then situational forces, and finally dispositions.

As he considers the second of these themes, Zimbardo revises the idiom of "a few bad apples." This traditional phrase states that every barrel of apples contains at least a few bad ones—and it is intended as a metaphor, implying that every group of people will contain a few bad people. The fact that this metaphor exists, according to Zimbardo, is evidence of people's tendency to assume that the primary cause of evil behavior is the individual's innate disposition. But he says, "The *bad apple-dispositional* view ignores the apple barrel and its potentially corrupting situational impact on those within it."[3]

Zimbardo prefers an analysis that focuses "on the barrel makers, on those with the power to design the barrel."[4] In place of the traditional idiom, he suggests a more reflective metaphor of bad barrels, rather than bad apples. Zimbardo writes that "barrel makers" can include nearly anyone with the power to shape situations and direct behavior: governments, corporate leaders, sports coaches, military leaders, religious leaders, and even Zimbardo himself, as lead experimenter in the SPE.

> *"One of the dominant conclusions of the Stanford Prison Experiment is that the pervasive yet subtle power of a host of situational variables can dominate an individual's will to resist."*
>
> —— Philip Zimbardo, *The Lucifer Effect: Understanding How Good People Turn Evil*

Exploring the Ideas

Many of the ideas and evidence behind Zimbardo's key themes come from the SPE. In this 1971 study, Zimbardo created a makeshift prison in the basement of Stanford University's psychology department and randomly assigned 24 young male volunteers the role of either prisoner or guard. Zimbardo, who played the role of prison superintendent, writes that randomly assigning participants to the role of guard "ensured that they were initially good apples and were corrupted by the insidious power of the bad barrel, this prison."[5]

In other words, both the prisoners and guards could have been considered interchangeable before the start of the study. Assuming power, based only on the randomness of their assignment to the role, the guards soon verbally abused prisoners, forced them into physical labor, intentionally disrupted their sleep, and secluded some into solitary confinement.*

The experiment was scheduled to last two weeks, but Zimbardo canceled it at the end of the first week after several prisoners became anguished at the physical and psychological abuse that the guards inflicted on them. Zimbardo recaps the effect that this abuse had on the prisoners, writing in *The Lucifer Effect*: "Half of our student prisoners had to be released early because of severe emotional and cognitive disorders."[6]

Zimbardo then applies his analysis to the prison abuse and torture that occurred at Abu Ghraib and claims that they parallel those found during the SPE, being only more atrocious in scale. Both instances were made possible, Zimbardo claims, because of situational and systemic factors.

Zimbardo describes many similar situational factors in both settings. He states that "boredom operated in both settings,"[7] that the guards were not properly trained, and that they had total power with little accountability. In relation to the wider systemic factors, Zimbardo argues that a "culture of abuse"[8] existed during the Iraq War,* facilitated by the US government and military command. He writes that they employed "torture tactics—under sanitized terms— and failed to provide the leadership, oversight, accountability, and mission-specific training necessary."[9] US government officials, for instance, framed the invasion of Iraq as part of their "war on terror"[10] and used the term "enhanced interrogation" rather than torture. From Zimbardo's perspective, such policies probably helped to normalize and justify the abuse of Iraqi prisoners.

Language and Expression

As labels for some of his main themes, Zimbardo used metaphors and idioms. The most prominent example of this is his reformulation of the bad apple metaphor to introduce the idea of bad barrels. Another is the title, *The Lucifer Effect*, which references the story of Lucifer* from Christian mythology. Lucifer was an angel of God who epitomized everything good and moral—before he fell from God's grace and transformed into the most evil of beings. Zimbardo asks his readers, "Could we, like God's favorite angel, Lucifer, ever be led into the temptation to do the unthinkable to others?"[11] Zimbardo's answer is a clear "yes," and the story of Lucifer serves as an apt example of this moral transformation. Although they are simplifications, the bad apple and Lucifer metaphors are useful entry points, and summaries, of Zimbardo's key themes.

Zimbardo devotes much of the text to the description of his 1971 Stanford Prison Experiment (SPE). He characterizes that as a "chapter-by-chapter chronology... presented in a cinematic format, as a personal narrative told in the present tense with minimal psychological interpretation."[12] As a result, this section is less academic and more dramatic than the rest of the text.

Zimbardo also includes transcripts of recordings of the experiment and segments from post-study interviews, which offer insightful evidence for many of his claims. One participant assigned as a guard described his experience: "My enjoyment in harassing and punishing prisoners was quite unnatural for me, because I tend to think of myself as being sympathetic to the injured, especially animals. I think that it was an outgrowth from my total freedom to rule the prisoners, I began to abuse my authority."[13] This participant's experience touches on the themes that Zimbardo championed: that in powerful situations, people's behavior may change in transformative, surprising, and even abusive ways.

1. Philip Zimbardo, *The Lucifer Effect: Understanding How Good People Turn Evil* (New York: Random House, 2007), vii.

2. Zimbardo, *Lucifer*, 3.

3. Zimbardo, *Lucifer*, 10.

4. Zimbardo, *Lucifer*, 10.

5. Zimbardo, *Lucifer*, 229.

6. Zimbardo, *Lucifer*, 196.

7. Zimbardo, *Lucifer*, 352.

8. Zimbardo, *Lucifer*, 377.

9. Zimbardo, *Lucifer*, 378.

10. Zimbardo, *Lucifer*, 378.

11. Zimbardo, *Lucifer*, xii.

12. Zimbardo, *Lucifer*, xii.

13. Zimbardo, *Lucifer*, 187.

MODULE 6
SECONDARY IDEAS

KEY POINTS

* *The Lucifer Effect's* secondary ideas include an examination of the psychological and social mechanisms responsible for people's turn to evil, as well as Philip Zimbardo's prescriptions for avoiding those pitfalls.

* Zimbardo describes group-based factors, such as the psychological desire to feel accepted by groups and the effect of feeling anonymous in groups, as mechanisms that lead people towards evil. To act heroically instead, one must be aware of, and combat, such factors.

* He also introduces a new idea in this text, examining how wider systems often facilitate the types of situations that are conducive to evil, and he discusses how these factors have been relatively overlooked.

Other Ideas

Philip Zimbardo's *The Lucifer Effect* contains two secondary ideas:
* A particular set of psychological and social mechanisms that push people to commit evil acts. He details what he views as the most prominent mechanisms.
* By consciously resisting those factors, people can become heroes—acting "on behalf of others, when yet others are doing evil or doing nothing to stop it."[1]

In his search for the psychological and social mechanisms that lead people to evil, Zimbardo draws on five decades of social psychological* research. He concludes that there are two distinct sets of factors. The first can be thought of as group-based factors, such as the need to belong and feel welcomed by a group. These group-based factors exist when there are at least two people, and they typically involve one or more people exerting an influence, such as peer pressure,* on others in the group. Zimbardo describes the power that these group-based factors wield, noting, "The imagined threat of being cast [out of one's group] can lead some people to do virtually anything to avoid their terrifying rejection."[2]

The second set can be thought of as anonymity factors, which Zimbardo says are "anything, or any situation, that makes people feel anonymous, as though no one knows who they are or cares to know."[3] The effect of such factors, he continues, reduces people's "sense of personal accountability, thereby creating the potential for evil action."[4] This effect is exemplified by communications over the Internet, which being often anonymous, can typically be less civil and more antagonistic than face-to-face communications.

Zimbardo's other secondary idea is that people can avoid these pitfalls just as, according to him, heroes do. In addition to viewing most people as capable of evil, he also thinks most people are capable of heroism. Referencing a phrase descriptive of the capacity for "normal" people to perform "evil" acts in a routine fashion, Zimbardo writes: "The banality of evil* shares much with the banality of heroism. Neither attribute is the direct consequence of unique dispositional* tendencies."[5] A person's individual characteristics, in other words, do not necessarily have too much to do with his or her capacity to act in an evil or heroic way.

Instead, he argues, heroes manage to sidestep the group-based and anonymity factors that often elicit evil in so many others.

> *"In contrast to the 'banality of evil,' which posits that ordinary people can be responsible for the most despicable acts of cruelty and degradation of their fellows, I posit the 'banality of heroism,' which unfurls the banner of the heroic Everyman and Everywoman, who heed the call to service to humanity when their time comes to act."*
>
> —— Philip Zimbardo, *The Lucifer Effect: Understanding How Good People Turn Evil*

Exploring the Ideas

According to Zimbardo, the first mechanisms that can elicit evil are the group-based psychological factors. He considers that the need to belong was a primary mechanism for the outcome of the Stanford Prison Experiment (SPE), writing, "The basic need to belong, to associate with and be accepted by others, so central to community building and family bonding, was diverted in the SPE into conformity* with newly emergent norms,* that enabled the guards to abuse the prisoners."[6] In psychology, "norms" refer to the accepted and expected standards, values, and ways to behave and think in any given group, and are defined by the group itself. In this way, Zimbardo explains that people are sometimes willing to forego their own moral instincts if, in return, they are accepted into a group that they wish, or feel obligated, to join.

In The *Lucifer Effect*, Zimbardo also considers other group-based factors such as conformity and obedience to authority.* He references the obedience studies* of the psychologist Stanley Milgram* in the 1960s as evidence of the profound effect that authorities have in convincing others to obey their commands. In those studies, an experimenter commanded study participants to provide simulated electrical shocks to strangers who provided incorrect responses to some task. Most participants in these Milgram studies administered the highest available levels of shock, despite protestations from those being shocked. Overall, such group-based factors involve a powerful leader or the group's norms swaying group members to act in ways that go against their personal moral standards.

The second set of mechanisms that Zimbardo says can elicit evil are factors serving anonymity. "Deindividuation"* is a psychological phenomenon according to which people feel such a sense of anonymity in a wider group that they lose their sense of self-awareness and personal responsibility—leading to behaviors that would otherwise be out of character.

Meanwhile, dehumanization* involves deliberately overlooking or devaluing the humanity of another person (or group), usually viewing and treating the dehumanized as lesser, unequal, or animal. As Zimbardo describes, dehumanizing is excluding others "from the moral order of being a human person."[7] He notes that the two processes are often in play in situations that elicit evil. In the SPE, for instance, the guards addressed all the prisoners by numerical IDs instead of their names, which served to dehumanize them. Meanwhile, they themselves wore matching opaque sunglasses and uniforms, which deindividuated them.

Regarding heroes, Zimbardo writes that they do not have "some inherent magical goodness but rather, more likely, an understanding, however intuitive, of mental and social tactics of resistance."[8] So just as Zimbardo argues that nearly everyone is capable of evil, he similarly argues that nearly everyone is capable of heroism. But to be heroic, one must be aware of the psychological and social influences that often lead to evil and find methods to avoid them. For instance, being aware of—and consciously accepting your responsibility for—your actions or inactions will combat the effects of situations causing deindividuation.

Overlooked

Although *The Lucifer Effect* is a relatively recent book (published in 2007), much of the research and ideas it contains come from earlier works by Zimbardo and others. Zimbardo admits, however, that he and his colleagues in the field had previously overlooked the psychological effect of the system* (meaning larger organizations, governments, and cultures) on eliciting evil and failed to explore its high-level ability to impact every situation.

Speaking of broader systems, Zimbardo writes that "most psychologists have been insensitive to the deeper sources of power [inherent in] the political, economic, religious, historic, and cultural matrix that defines situations."[9] In his view, his academic peers were successful in examining how situations—such as a prison, school, church, or a simple collection of individuals—can influence behavior. But those researchers had consistently neglected to consider how such groups are created in the real world and the power that creators of such situations have.

For instance, in *The Lucifer Effect*, Zimbardo specifically blames US President George W. Bush,* Vice President Dick Cheney,* Defense Secretary Donald Rumsfeld,* and several other military leaders holding power at the time of the Abu Ghraib* prison abuses. He points out their role in establishing and enabling a culture that developed the "bad barrel"[10] that led to the torture at Abu Ghraib.

Previously, social psychologists have considered analyses at the level of the system to be generally outside the scope of their field, presuming them to be the remit of sociologists (those who study human society), political scientists (those who study the nature and actions of political systems and participants in those systems), and economists. Zimbardo's focus on systems is one of the newer ideas in *The Lucifer Effect*, so it remains to be seen to what extent psychologists will consider variables at the level of the system in the future—at least when examining the roots of situations that elicit unethical behavior.

1. Philip Zimbardo, *The Lucifer Effect: Understanding How Good People Turn Evil* (New York: Random House, 2007), viii.
2. Zimbardo, *Lucifer*, 259.
3. Zimbardo, *Lucifer*, 301.
4. Zimbardo, *Lucifer*, 301.
5. Zimbardo, *Lucifer*, 485.

6. Zimbardo, *Lucifer*, 258.

7. Zimbardo, *Lucifer*, 307.

8. Zimbardo, *Lucifer*, xiii.

9. Zimbardo, *Lucifer*, x.

10. Zimbardo, *Lucifer*, x.

MODULE 7
ACHIEVEMENT

KEY POINTS

* In *The Lucifer Effect*, Philip Zimbardo provides the most extensive telling and analysis of the Stanford Prison Experiment (SPE),* and he uses this analysis to explain the situational forces* involved in the Abu Ghraib* prison scandal.

* As the Abu Ghraib abuses and Zimbardo's involvement in the trial of one guard are both relatively recent events, the text is timely and revealing.

* The reliability of the SPE, and the universality of its findings, are difficult to demonstrate because ethical considerations largely prevent replication of the original study.

Assessing the Argument

In his review of Philip Zimbardo's *The Lucifer Effect: Understanding How Good People Turn Evil*, the social psychologist Robert Levine* asks, "Why a new book about a 35-year-old study?"[1] He answers his own question, writing, "[Zimbardo] provides a wealth of new interpretations and new material—anecdotes, entries from the diaries of prisoners and guards, updates on the lives of the participants, and documentation of the consequences his findings have had for real-world prison policy."[2]

Examples are Zimbardo's presentations of his findings directly to judicial and law enforcement groups as well as his testimony in court, arguing that solitary confinement* of prisoners is psychologically damaging and abusive.

Although Zimbardo's analyses of heroism and how systemic factors (such as governments) enable powerful situations are somewhat less comprehensive, they nevertheless provide a valuable starting point for further investigation. Zimbardo notes in *The Lucifer Effect* that social psychologists have largely ignored the topics of heroism and systemic influences on behavior, and he hopes he can stimulate future research on the topics. Levine praised Zimbardo's work on heroism and his nuanced definition and categorization of heroic thought and behaviors, adding that he hoped it "will stimulate long-overdue research and education in this area."[3]

Although the topic remains largely ignored by researchers, Zimbardo is doing his part to educate the world with his Heroic Imagination Project (HIP),* a public training program that teaches people how to avoid potential pitfalls that prevent heroic acts. Those include deindividuation* (the loss of a sense of one's own self and tendencies due to inclusion in a group or because of one's anonymity), dehumanization* (overlooking or devaluing the human attributes of another person), and conformity* (matching one's thought and behavior to that of a group due to things such as social pressure).

> *"Drawing on path-breaking experimental work conducted in the 1970s in the Stanford Prison Experiment, Zimbardo brilliantly examines the current Abu Ghraib prison torture scandal. He meticulously details the situational factors which can make good people engage in evil acts, in order to meet natural and normal human needs for safety, knowledge, and affection."*
>
> ——Rose McDermott, "Reviewed Work: *The Lucifer Effect: Understanding How Good People Turn Evil* by Philip Zimbardo"

Achievement in Context

Although the SPE study is more than three decades old, the events at Abu Ghraib acted as an impetus for Zimbardo and made a retelling of the study more relevant and instructive than ever. In her review of *The Lucifer Effect*, the political scientist Rose McDermott* said that the SPE remains "hauntingly relevant upon the release of the photos from Abu Ghraib prison some 30 years later."[4] She noted that the text "contains many photos from the original experiment, and they will strike any viewer as startlingly familiar in design to the more recent Abu Ghraib pictures. Some of the poses in which guards placed prisoners reemerge as identical in nature and scope."[5]

Even the 2004 Schlesinger report,* the independent report of the Abu Ghraib abuses that was commissioned by the US Department of Defense (DoD), noted the relevance, stating, "The landmark Stanford study provides a cautionary tale for all military detention operations."[6] Some observers may have expected that the Schlesinger report would influence US policy on the treatment of foreign military prisoners and terror suspects, given the report's official status and the amount of media attention it attracted. However, later reports (including one of 2010 by Amnesty International,* an organization founded to defend the human rights of political prisoners) found that the US government's abuse and torture of detainees continued in other prisons for years after the publication of the Schlesinger report and *The Lucifer Effect*. Abu Ghraib, however, was closed in 2008.

Limitations

The psychologist Stanley Milgram's* obedience studies* and Zimbardo's SPE most vividly demonstrate the possible magnitude of unexpected and evil behaviors. However, they are not often replicated because of ethical considerations, as they both placed participants in scenarios that are today deemed too psychologically stressful to repeat. Thus, it is difficult to prove the universality of the power of situations.

Social psychologists have also noted that people's perceptions of the power of situations are culturally variable. Zimbardo writes in his text: "The traditional view (among those who come from cultures that emphasize individualism)* is to look within for answers—for pathology or heroism. Modern psychiatry is dispositionally* oriented."[7] In other words, in some "individualist" cultures, such as in Western countries like the United States, people tend to think of themselves as individuals more than as members of a group. As a result, they generally tend to attribute the cause of events to innate personality factors (or "dispositions.") Therefore, it's assumed that a person's aggressive act is most likely evidence that he or she is an aggressive person rather than the result of some situational factor.

Zimbardo points out that a willingness to assume the "bad apple" explanation for unethical acts might vary by culture, with American and Western culture in particular likely to rely on the bad apple attributions. In non-Western cultures, such as in East Asia, people are often more attuned to situational factors and the influence they have on people's lives. The consequence of this is that Western, individualist cultures, at least according to Zimbardo's view, are less likely to notice and question authorities that may be enabling bad situations, like their government or their boss.

An additional limitation to the text is Zimbardo's reluctance to define what he means by "evil." He instead provides many examples of what he considers to be evil—from the guards' behaviors during the SPE and at Abu Ghraib to cases of financial fraud, genocide, and sexual abuse. Zimbardo notes that he views evil as broader than what in his opinion is typically described as such, and he writes that it is more than "political leaders who have orchestrated mass murders."[8] It seems that Zimbardo intends to consider evil as a broad category with unclear boundaries. But he does not address in the text the likelihood that different people and societies will differ in what they consider evil.

---

1. Robert Levine, "The Evil That Men Do," *American Scientist*, September-October 2007, accessed September 15, 2015, http://www. americanscientist.org/bookshelf/content2/2007/5/the-evil-that-men-do.

2. Robert Levine, "The Evil That Men Do."

3. Robert Levine, "The Evil That Men Do."

4. Rose McDermott, "Reviewed Work: *The Lucifer Effect: Understanding How Good People Turn Evil* by Philip Zimbardo," 645.

5. McDermott, "Reviewed Work," 645.

6. Philip Zimbardo, *The Lucifer Effect: Understanding How Good People Turn Evil* (New York: Random House, 2007), 324.

7. Zimbardo, *Lucifer*, 7.

8. Zimbardo, *Lucifer*, 6.

MODULE 8
PLACE IN THE AUTHOR'S WORK

KEY POINTS

* One of Philip Zimbardo's interests lies in examining when and how people act unexpectedly. In the 1971 Stanford Prison Experiment (SPE)* and *The Lucifer Effect* (2007), this involves supposedly ordinary people acting out evil.

* Though his research based on the SPE has laid out a prototype for the power of the situation,* Zimbardo's other work has been more reliant on dispositional* factors—those associated with the individual's personality.

* The publication of *The Lucifer Effect*, however, has reignited the original debates prompted by the SPE during the 1970s. As a result, the book has reaffirmed Zimbardo's reputation for research on situations.

Positioning

Published in 2007, *The Lucifer Effect: Understanding How Good People Turn Evil* is a late publication in Philip Zimbardo's career. However, it relies on work conducted during the early stages of his career and serves as a return to the research topics with which he has been most associated: the power of the situation, evil behavior, and the dynamics and psychological consequences of imprisonment. Relatively new in *The Lucifer Effect* is Zimbardo's consideration of systemic* factors and his focus on heroism* through avoiding negative situational forces.*

Zimbardo admits in the book that for much of his career, he overlooked the influence of systems such as institutions. In an interview, he noted that he was "unaware even with the Stanford prison study about the power of the system, because I was the system."[1] He says that he only had this realization while serving as expert witness for the American soldier Ivan Frederick,* accused of mistreating detainees at the Abu Ghraib* prison in 2004.

Above all, *The Lucifer Effect* marks Zimbardo's transition toward what has since become his primary focus: heroism. Although he only discusses heroism in a short section of the book, it has served as a catalyst for his later focus on heroism. In 2010, Zimbardo launched the Heroic Imagination Project (HIP)* which trains interested participants to resist negative situational factors. He writes that this "lies in development of the three Ss: self-awareness, situational sensitivity, and street smarts."[2] All three involve first understanding the power of negative situational factors, such as deindividuation* and conformity* and then thinking about how one might react to those pressures. Thus, the premise of Zimbardo's HIP had its origins in *The Lucifer Effect*.

> "At the core of my interest is the process of transformation of human nature.What factors account for how we suddenly change, how we act in ways that are not based on what we did before, or on what we thought we knew about ourselves and about other people?"
>
> —— Philip Zimbardo in an interview by Christina Maslach,
> *Emperor of the Edge*

Integration

Although Zimbardo remains most associated with the SPE and a "situationist"* school of thought (focusing on the power of the situation), he has covered a range of research topics throughout his career. In fact, he describes himself as a generalist in psychology rather than a specialist in any one area. Nonetheless, some broad themes run through his body of work.

In one interview, he described his core interest, saying, "I have been primarily interested in how and why ordinary people do unusual things, things that seem alien to their natures."³ Two of his other key research interests have been shyness and the perception of time. In his work on shyness, Zimbardo strives to help shy people overcome their lack of confidence and, in a sense, behave in ways that are unusual for them. However, counter to the stance found in *The Lucifer Effect* and his other research on evil, Zimbardo's shyness work tends to focus more on dispositions. He sees shyness as a personality variable, or the result of thinking styles, rather than the result of situational factors alone.

Zimbardo's research on time perspective also provides additional nuance to his body of work. It details how a person's emphasis—or overemphasis—on events of the past, possibilities for the future, or living in the present moment can affect their behaviors. This work is what psychologists might call interactionist* as it considers that the *interaction* between a person's personality and the situation is a better predictor of behavior than either the personality element or the situation element on its own.

Zimbardo explicitly regards time perspective in this way, writing that he considers it "as situationally determined and as a relatively stable individual-differences process."[4] (More simply put, he means that both situational and dispositional factors are integral to people's perception of time.) As a result, although Zimbardo's position as a situationist is obvious in his writings on the SPE and *The Lucifer Effect*, his work in social psychology* has been more varied and nuanced, including both dispositional and interactionist ideas.

Significance

Based on two key events to which Zimbardo had unique access, *The Lucifer Effect* is probably his most extensive and detailed work, as well as most widely accessible text. It also assigns more blame and offers up more prescriptions than any of his previous works, largely directed at the US military and government. For instance, Zimbardo assigns specific blame to former US President George W. Bush* and Secretary of Defense Donald Rumsfeld* for their roles in establishing a large-scale system that ultimately dehumanized* Iraqis (that is, robbed them of their status as human beings).

The Lucifer Effect has further cemented Zimbardo's association with the SPE and his position as a situationist. Both have been controversial topics since Zimbardo's original work in the 1970s, and this text has reignited some of those debates—with Zimbardo again becoming a central and polarizing figure. While the SPE is held as one of the most famous, interesting and possibly informative studies in the field, it is also regarded as one of the most unethical. Zimbardo has acknowledged this many times in his career, including in *The Lucifer Effect*, in which he asks the question: "Was the SPE unethical? In several ways, the answer must surely be 'Yes.'"[5]

Nonetheless, Zimbardo qualifies his admission, arguing that the study was not unethical by other standards. He also claims the presumed suffering of the SPE participants was acceptable and worthwhile. While the text provides much new detail into one of the field's seminal studies as well as new ideas about systemic factors and heroism, it has also vaulted Zimbardo back into a debate over ethics in the field. For some observers, this invariably colors his reputation.

---

1. Marina Krakovsky, "Zimbardo Unbound," *Stanford Magazine*, May/June 2007, accessed September 27, 2015, https://alumni.stanford.edu/get/page/magazine/article/?article_id=32541.

2. Philip Zimbardo, *The Lucifer Effect: Understanding How Good People Turn Evil* (New York: Random House, 2007), 452.

3. Christina Maslach, "Emperor of the Edge," *Psychology Today*, September 1, 2000, accessed September 15, 2015, https://www.psychologytoday.com/articles/200009/emperor-the-edge.

4. Philip G. Zimbardo, and John N. Boyd, "Putting Time in Perspective: A Valid, Reliable Individual-Differences Metric." *Journal of Personality and Social Psychology* 77, no. 6 (1999): 1272.

5. Zimbardo, *Lucifer*, 231.

SECTION 3
IMPACT

THE FIRST RESPONSES

KEY POINTS

- The prominent feature of Philip Zimbardo's *The Lucifer Effect*, the Stanford Prison Experiment (SPE),* has long been criticized as unethical and methodologically suspect.

- Zimbardo concedes that the SPE included lapses in ethical practice; however he defends his original analysis of the study against methodological critiques.

- The SPE became a seminal case study in ethics for the field, and the 2007 release of *The Lucifer Effect* reignited debate over Zimbardo's interpretation of the study's results.

Criticism

Because Philip Zimbardo's *The Lucifer Effect: Understanding How Good People Turn Evil* relies so heavily on the Stanford Prison Experiment, criticisms of the text mostly reflect the original criticisms of the 1971 study. These tend to focus on two main concerns: ethics and methodology. One 1973 reviewer was particularly critical regarding the ethics of the study, claiming that participants were not provided with enough accurate information in advance to consent to the experiment and that their suffering was not justified.

Nearly four decades later, a reviewer of *The Lucifer Effect* noted that the SPE was "now used as a case study of research ethics gone awry."[1] Zimbardo's SPE participants endured more psychological distress than most social scientists felt was acceptable. Critics also argued that because Zimbardo acted as superintendent of the makeshift prison, he was unable to objectively monitor the condition and safety of participants.

In the first years after the SPE, criticisms of its methodology focused on alternative explanations for the events that took place. Many people believed that the participants' behaviors were not as organic as Zimbardo suggested. A common critique was that of political scientist Ali Banuazizi* and the sociologist* Siamak Movahedi.* In 1975, they wrote that demand characteristics* were largely responsible for the events that took place during the SPE.

The term "demand characteristics" refers to a situation where participants form their own interpretation of the purpose of the experiment or the expectations of the experimenter. Thus, feeling an implicit pressure to perform as expected, they subconsciously change their behavior to fit that interpretation.This creates a bias in the results and serious questions about the validity of any observed effects.

Banuazizi and Movahedi argued that the participants probably uncovered Zimbardo's hypothesis and expectations for the study, and they may have adapted their behaviors to please him. Banuazizi and Movahedi noted that "the subjects entered the experiment carrying strong social stereotypes of how guards and prisoners act and relate to one another in a real prison,"[2] and they essentially acted out those roles.

"Was the SPE [Stanford Prison Experiment] study unethical? No and Yes. No, because it followed the guidelines of the Human Subjects Research Review Board* that reviewed it and approved it... Yes, it was unethical because people suffered and others were allowed to inflict pain and*

humiliation on their fellows over an extended period of time."
——— Philip Zimbardo et al., *Reflections on the Stanford Prison Experiment: Genesis, Transformations, Consequences*

Responses

Since the publication of *The Lucifer Effect*, Zimbardo seems to have avoided making any public responses to such criticisms. In 2007, he published a short post on his website to those with any concerns over the book's conclusions or any renewed doubts about the SPE's methodology, writing: "I do not have the time nor the inclination to enter into any further discussion or debate about this matter."[3] He probably did not consider it worthwhile to repeat the stance that he had provided in previous years, particularly as *The Lucifer Effect* included the original responses to these criticisms.

For instance, Zimbardo had conceded in 1973 that in some ways the study was unethical. But he also defended himself on several grounds, noting that he had gained approval from several institutional review boards* to conduct the study. He also argued that he debriefed* his participants many times (in a post-study discussion which gives participants additional information about the study and checks for any psychological strain). Zimbardo noted that he disclosed the true intent of the work and was "sufficiently convinced that the suffering we observed, and were responsible for, was stimulus-bound [that is, a specific behavior that occurs as a response to a specific stimuli] and did not extend beyond the confines of that basement prison."[4]

He repeats those arguments in *The Lucifer Effect*, saying that while, in absolute terms, the study was unethical, enough was learned from it to warrant the strain it placed on its participants. Zimbardo declares: "On the relativist side of the ethical argument [that is, making judgments based on the relative value of costs and benefits, rather than on absolute truths or values], one could contend that the SPE was not unethical."[5]

However, Zimbardo does admit in the book that some demand characteristics were likely to be present. He writes about his own role adoption and acting during the study, noting: "In retrospect, my role transformation from usually compassionate teacher to data-focused researcher to callous prison superintendent was most distressing."[6]

Zimbardo, however, offers a different interpretation. He contends that this only further illustrates the power of the situation*—in that it changed even him—rather than being evidence that he or the participants were intentionally acting out roles.

Conflict and Consensus

In response to the immediate criticisms of the SPE in 1971 and those that have continued up to—and even after—the publication of *The Lucifer Effect*, Zimbardo has stuck to his original interpretation of the SPE's findings and maintained the same responses to questions about the study's ethics. There seems to be little movement on the side of Zimbardo's critics, as well. They consider the SPE, alongside Stanley Milgrim's* 1960s obedience studies,* as social psychology's* prime examples of unethical research.

In their influential 2012 handbook on research ethics, the psychologist Joan E. Sieber* and sociologist Martin B. Tolich* argue that "Zimbardo's ethical problem stemmed from... [his] conflict of interest as a researcher... and a co-subject in his role as prison superintendent."[7] They write that the SPE is now informative, suggesting: "All researchers can take lessons from this conflict of interest. Researchers... need to monitor the study and the subjects at all times."[8] In other words, they maintain that, as prison superintendent, Zimbardo could not objectively monitor the safety of the study participants and, on that point, Zimbardo agrees.

Questions over both the role of demand characteristics in the SPE study and challenges to the interpretations of Zimbardo's analysis have also persisted, although no consensus has been reached. Zimbardo continues to defend his original interpretation of the SPE and now its application to other events, such as the Abu Ghraib* prison abuses. Meanwhile, the release of *The Lucifer Effect* has caused renewed interest in finding alternative explanations for the SPE.

1. Wray Herbert, "The Banality of Evil," *Observer*, April 2007, accessed September 27, 2015, http://aps.psychologicalscience.org/index.php/publications/observer/2007/april-07/the-banality-of-evil.html.

2. Ali Banuazizi and Siamak Movahedi, "Interpersonal Dynamics in a Simulated Prison: A Methodological Analysis," *American Psychologist* 30, no. 2 (1975): 156.

3. Philip Zimbardo, "Person X Situation X System Dynamics," *The Lucifer Effect*, accessed September 27, 2015, http://www.lucifereffect.com/apsrejoinder.htm.

4. Philip G. Zimbardo, "On the Ethics of Intervention in Human Psychological Research: With Special Reference to the Stanford Prison Experiment," *Cognition* 2, no. 2 (1973): 254.

5. Philip Zimbardo, *The Lucifer Effect: Understanding How Good People Turn Evil* (New York: Random House, 2007), 263.

6. Zimbardo, *Lucifer*, 218.

7. Joan E. Sieber and Martin B. Tolich, *Planning Ethically Responsible Research* (Thousand Oaks: Sage Publications, 2012), 67.

8. Sieber and Tolich, *Responsible*, 67.

MODULE 10
THE EVOLVING DEBATE

KEY POINTS

- *The Lucifer Effect* provides arguments and evidence that certain settings, such as US prisons, are likely to be home to abuse, sadism,* and evil.

- *The Lucifer Effect* established a school of thought that bad situations create bad people. Another school of thought countered that it is bad people in a situation that make it bad.

- The Stanford Prison Experiment (SPE)* and *The Lucifer Effect* have particularly influenced research on prison settings.

Uses and Problems

The ideas found in Philip Zimbardo's 2007 *The Lucifer Effect: Understanding How Good People Turn Evil* have influenced academic literature on prison policy. The social psychologist* Craig Haney* argues that evidence from the SPE and other prison research demonstrates that, "because of their harmful potential, prisons should be deployed very sparingly in the war on crime."[1] A psychology professor at the University of California, Santa Cruz, Haney is renowned for his work on the psychological effects of incarceration and the effectiveness of prisons. The crux of his argument is that if prisons have the capability to alter people's behavior, as demonstrated by the SPE, this power ought to be used to rehabilitate inmates. Yet, as the SPE and other prison research has documented, prisons are instead more likely to dehumanize* and even psychologically torture inmates.

Despite its influence on prison policy, the release of *The Lucifer Effect* also led to the continuation of—and increase in— concerns surrounding Zimbardo's methodology and interpretation of the SPE. In 2001, Stephen Reicher* and S. Alexander Haslam,* both social psychologists and psychology professors, conducted one notable study in collaboration with the BBC* (the British Broadcasting Corporation). The researchers randomly split 15 participants into prisoner and guard groups in a makeshift detention center. This was not, however, a replication of the SPE—partly because it would be forbidden by modern ethics. In this instance, Reicher and Haslam reported that guards were "reluctant to impose their authority and they were eventually overcome by the prisoners."[2] The remainder of the study included participants attempting to form an egalitarian* structure, where all people are treated equally, by fairly delegating various tasks and chores. But this approach failed and was supplanted by efforts to reestablish a guard-prisoner hierarchy.

> "The potential for significant abuse [is inherent in] the very structure of a prison. Whatever its limitations as a literal simulation of an actual prison setting, the venerable Stanford Prison Experiment demonstrated the potentially destructive dynamic that is created whenever near absolute power is wielded over a group of derogated [that is, insulted and treated as worthless] and vilified others."
>
> —— Craig Haney, *A Culture of Harm Taming the Dynamics of Cruelty in Supermax Prisons*

Schools of Thought

This BBC prison study* and other alternative explanations of the SPE have led to a more nuanced school of thought on the power of situations.* Zimbardo has advocated a cause-and-effect process, arguing that difficult situations and systems (bad barrels) create bad apples. But the BBC prison study suggests that powerful situations such as prisons descending into sadism and evil are less inevitable than Zimbardo suggests.

Reicher and Haslam argue that "the way in which members of strong groups behave depends upon the norms* and values associated with their specific social identity and may be either anti-or prosocial."[3] This argument suggests, in part, that Zimbardo developed and enabled a situation in the SPE prison that promoted abuse, and that Zimbardo, more than the situational factors he detailed, was responsible for the outcomes of the SPE.

Further work has suggested that it is more likely that "bad apples" create the "bad barrels." In 2007, psychology professors Thomas Carnahan* and Sam McFarland* conducted a study that aimed to examine the personality characteristics of people who respond to recruitment materials requesting participants for a prison study. They found that "volunteers who responded to a newspaper ad to participate in a psychological study of prison life, an ad virtually identical to that used in the Stanford Prison Experiment,"[4] were higher on several measures of aggression and had a greater tendency to support authority and social dominance than people responding to a hypothetical study with a parallel advert omitting the words "prison life."[5]

This school of thought fits into the interactionist* category, as it not only gives similar weight to personality* and situational* factors in determining behavior but it also suggests that the interaction between certain personalities in certain situations can be better predictors of behavior than personalities or situations on their own. Those personalities are, for example, people with authoritarian* personalities—those given to the exercise of their authority—in a strongly hierarchical systems like a prison.

In Current Scholarship

In addition to the academic debates in the fields of social and personality psychology* that the text has spurred, Craig Haney—one of Zimbardo's former students who acted as a key researcher during the SPE—has become a leading voice in prison research and prison policy. Haney wrote in 2008 that "we have reached the upper limit of the psychological, social, economic, and even cultural costs that our society can afford to incur in the name of this commitment to inflicting penal pain."[6] His conclusions are based on decades of research that largely began with his involvement in the SPE and are in line with Zimbardo's analysis of the SPE and its implications for prison policy.

Haney has found that the psychological strain and suffering that occurred during the SPE is much worse in actual prisons. This suffering is due to many factors that were apparent in the SPE, such as the isolation of prisoners, power abuses in prisons, and the emphasis on punishment rather than rehabilitation.

Starting in the 1970s, the US began a "'get tough' approach to crime control,"[7] with the expansion of prisons and lengthening of prison sentences. Haney writes that these prison policies and practices have since "crossed the line from inflicting pain to doing real harm—at a societal as well as individual level."[8] America incarcerates a significant segment of the population, and rather than rehabilitating criminals, the system does them additional psychological harm before sending them back into society at the end of their prison sentence.

1. Craig Haney and Philip Zimbardo, "The Past and Future of US Prison Policy: Twenty-five Years after the Stanford Prison Experiment." *American Psychologist* 53, no. 7 (1998): 719.

2. Stephen Reicher and S. Alexander Haslam, "Rethinking the Psychology of Tyranny: The BBC Prison Study." *British Journal of Social Psychology* 45, no. 1 (2006): 1.

3. Reicher and Haslam, "Tyranny," 33.

4. Thomas Carnahan and Sam McFarland, "Revisiting the Stanford Prison Experiment: Could Participant Self-Selection Have Led to the Cruelty?" *Personality and Social Psychology Bulletin* 33, no. 5 (2007): 610.

5. Carnahan and McFarland, "Revisiting," 610.

6. Craig Haney, "Counting Casualties in the War on Prisoners." *USFL* Rev. 43 (2008): 89.

7. Haney, "Prisoners," 88.

8. Haney, "Prisoners," 89.

MODULE 11
IMPACT AND INFLUENCE TODAY

KEY POINTS

* *The Lucifer Effect* today serves as the best record of the famous Stanford Prison Experiment (SPE).* It stands as a source of renewed controversy over both the SPE and the influence of situational forces* in eliciting unethical behavior. It is also the primary source for Philip Zimbardo's more recent ideas on systemic* causes of both behavior and heroism.*

* Zimbardo has since not participated in the ongoing debate over reinterpretations of the SPE and the power of situations.* Instead he has focused his attention on new work, primarily on heroism.

* Both social psychologists* and personality psychologists* continue to debate the power of situations to elicit unethical behavior.

Position

Philip Zimbardo's *The Lucifer Effect: Understanding How Good People Turn Evil* (2007) is the most comprehensive telling and analysis of the 1971 Stanford Prison Experiment to date. As such, it is historically relevant for the field of social psychology and is likely to remain so for some time.

The inclusion of so much new information on the SPE has also provided both sides with new material to debate. This includes previously unreleased transcripts from the study, photographs, and descriptions of video footage. In one post-study interview, a guard summarized his surprise at his behavior: "[When] a prisoner reacted violently toward me, I found that I had to defend myself, not as me but as me the guard... He hated me as the guard. He was reacting to the uniform. I had no choice but to defend myself as a guard."[1]

Such insights provide evidence for several of Zimbardo's contentions, such as people's adoption of roles (here as a guard) and their ability to deindividuate* (here the guard implying that the "true him" was not hated; it was "the guard").

To date, most attention to the text has focused on the continued debate over the power of situations and differing interpretations of the SPE. But some conversations now focus on the two newer topics contained in *The Lucifer Effect*. The first is Zimbardo's claim that wider systems produced the various bad situations described in the book. The second is his analysis of heroism as resulting from an awareness of, and ability to avoid, the pressures and pitfalls of bad situations.

These points reposition Zimbardo, who has moved away from his earlier work on the SPE, and they also involve new prescriptions and a new audience. Reviewing the book, the political scientist* Rose McDermott* summarized it as encouraging readers to resist "the subtle ways politicians and others use the environment to manipulate unsuspecting bystanders into doing their dirty work for them."[2] The idea, as promoted by Zimbardo, is that there is value in people questioning the intentions of their governments.

> "Bad apples vs. bad barrels' was the wrong way to frame this discussion. The metaphor oversimplifies a complex and troubling reality, which is that there is plenty of blame to go around."
>
> —— George R. Mastroianni, *Looking Back: Understanding Abu Ghraib*

Interaction

Zimbardo remains the most prominent voice promoting the ideas found in *The Lucifer Effect*. In recent years, he has apparently chosen to not get involved in the debate over the methodology of his work and the degree of situational factors at play in events such as the SPE and Abu Ghraib.* In 2007, Zimbardo stated on his website that these debates distract from the factors he hoped to focus on in *The Lucifer Effect*. He wrote that "while personality and social psychologists spar about the relative contributions of dispositions* and situations, we have ignored the most significant factor in the behavioral equation—the System."[3]

Thus, Zimbardo seems to be focusing now on the most recent of his themes in *The Lucifer Effect*: the effects of systems on human behavior and on heroism. This is a recent challenge to the fields of social psychology and personality psychology, with Zimbardo considering that enough work has been done on the power of situations and hoping to move into more positive, and applied, work on heroism. In a 2011 article, he wrote: "What makes us good? What makes us evil? Research has uncovered many answers to the second question... But when we ask why people become heroic, research doesn't yet have an answer."[4] It seems that, following *The Lucifer Effect*, Zimbardo has quickly shifted his focus from the predictors of evil to the predictors of heroism.

The Continuing Debate

However, those challenged by Zimbardo have not abandoned the debate over the influence of situational factors. In 2007, dozens of social and personality psychologists, several among the most respected in the world, wrote a letter to the Association for Psychological Science,* a major American psychology research organization, voicing concerns over *The Lucifer Effect*. "In contrast to Zimbardo," they wrote, "we believe that there is actually little scientific evidence indicating that situations are more important than dispositions for explaining behavior."[5] They also questioned the likelihood of Zimbardo's situational account of the abuses at Abu Ghraib.

Similarly, in a reanalysis of the SPE and Stanley Milgram's obedience studies,* the social psychologists Stephen Reicher* and S. Alexander Haslam* filmed a documentary reinterpretation of the SPE with volunteers that was broadcast on the British Broadcasting Corporation (BBC).* They maintained that a large body of research did not support the idea that situations can lead a majority of people to conform to evil.

Reicher and Haslam argued that the persistent "situationist"* idea ignores evidence that many people do resist the situational forces that Zimbardo described, and that those who do give in to situational pressures and "heed authority in doing evil do so knowingly not blindly, actively not passively, creatively not automatically... In short, they should be seen—and judged—as engaged followers not as blind conformists."[6] Thus, Reicher and Haslam contended that it is not ordinary people who are swayed by situations to evil, as Zimbardo argues, but rather people with a propensity for evil who are swayed by the situation.

1. Philip Zimbardo, *The Lucifer Effect: Understanding How Good People Turn Evil* (New York: Random House, 2007), 189.

2. Rose McDermott, "Reviewed Work: *The Lucifer Effect: Understanding How Good People Turn Evil* by Philip Zimbardo," Political Psychology 28, No. 5 (2007): 646.

3. Philip Zimbardo, "Person X Situation X System Dynamics," *The Lucifer Effect*, accessed September 27, 2015, http://www.lucifereffect.com/apsrejoinder.htm.

4. Philip Zimbardo, "What Makes a Hero?" *Greater Good Science Center*, January 18, 2011, accessed September 27, 2015, http://greatergood. berkeley.edu/article/item/what_makes_a_hero/.

5. M. Brent Donnellan et al., "Not So Situational," *Observer*, June/July 2007, accessed September 27, 2015, http://www.psychologicalscience.org/index. php/publications/observer/2007/june-july-07/not-so-situational.html.

6. S. Alexander Haslam and Stephen D. Reicher, "Contesting the 'Nature' Of Conformity: What Milgram and Zimbardo's Studies Really Show," *PLoS Biology* 10, no. 11 (2012): 1.

WHERE NEXT?

KEY POINTS

- *The Lucifer Effect* is likely to continue spurring controversy over interpretations of the Stanford Prison Experiment (SPE)* and the power of situations* to elicit unethical behavior. However, it also has the potential to serve as an inspiration for new work on heroism.*

- In the near future, Philip Zimbardo is most likely to carry out this potential through missions such as his Heroic Imagination Project.*

- The text is seminal for many reasons, including its dramatic and extensive retelling of one of psychology's most famed studies.

Potential

Philip Zimbardo's 1971 Stanford Prison Experiment and his 2007 book, *The Lucifer Effect: Understanding How Good People Turn Evil*, will continue to serve as a case study for research ethics and as a centerpiece in the debate over the situational determinants of behaviors. "Psychologists will find a wealth of fascinating new information in a nearly hour-by-hour account of the Stanford study,"[1] writes the psychology professor George R. Mastroianni.* He also suggests that "Zimbardo has made a major contribution to the field by including this new information, which will hopefully stimulate a significant reconsideration of the lessons of the Stanford study."[2]

Indeed, the few years since the text's release have seen a

renewed focus on the SPE and even on Stanley Milgram's* related obedience studies.* Though this renewed debate was not Zimbardo's intent with the book, and he has expressed disappointment over its persistence, the debate has already resulted in a more nuanced perspective of evil.

Zimbardo has been able to apply his ideas on heroism, and this work is likely to expand in the coming years. Chief among such early applications is a nonprofit organization that he established, the Heroic Imagination Project (HIP), which intends to teach "people how to take effective action in challenging situations."[3] Zimbardo has written that this project aims to conduct and encourage future research into the topic of heroism as well as to provide "research-based education and training programs for middle and high schools, corporations, and the military that make people aware of the social factors that produce passivity, inspire them to take positive civic action, and encourage the skills needed to consistently translate heroic impulses into action."[4]

> "Building on these insights, I have helped to start a program designed to learn more of heroism and to create the heroes of tomorrow."
>
> ——Philip Zimbardo, *What Makes a Hero?*

Future Directions

Zimbardo continues today as the most vocal, visible, and prominent thinker promoting the power of the situation*—specifically its ability to lead ordinary people to commit evil and to therefore serve as an explanation for many historical atrocities. He is also likely to continue as the most visible researcher promoting the ideas of heroism found in the text.

However, one of his former students, the clinical psychologist Zeno Franco,* has researched the topic of heroism alongside Zimbardo and is now an advisor to Zimbardo's Heroic Imagination Project. Writing in 2006, Franco wrote that having a "heroic imagination"[5] was an early candidate as a predictor and determinant of heroism, which he defined as "the capacity to imagine facing physically or socially risky situations, to struggle with the hypothetical problems these situations generate, and to consider one's actions and the consequences."[6] In essence, thinking through these possibilities before they occur can better prepare people for when they do occur.

Meanwhile, the social psychologist Craig Haney* is likely to continue researching US prison policies and advocating for prison reform. Many social scientists who are researching prisons acknowledge that US policy leaders have largely discounted their work. Yet Haney remains optimistic that both his research and the broader evidence from both prison research and social psychology* will eventually influence US public and political opinion about the role of prisons in society. He wrote in his 2005 book that the costs of the US policy of mass incarceration* is "beginning to register and mount in significant and unsettling ways in many communities across the country... there is a growing sense that it is time to seriously rethink what we have done."[7] Haney and other prison policy researchers typically hope for an approach to criminal justice that more effectively rehabilitates criminals, avoids the psychological damage associated with current US prisons, and does so for less money than the current rate of mass incarceration requires.

Summary

The Lucifer Effect offers the most readable and extensive report of one of the most famous psychology studies, the Stanford Prison Experiment. This alone makes it a valuable read for students. Yet the text offers much more, including a detailed analysis of many powerful social and group pressures, such as conformity* and deindividualization,* that are integral to understanding Zimbardo's take on the power of the situation. Even if a reader is skeptical of this power, the phenomena that Zimbardo presents are crucial to understanding the field of social psychology. And because such forces have the potential to influence behavior in ways that most people find objectionable, many people should find the book enlightening. It offers insights into tragic events such as Abu Ghraib* that many readers might otherwise have difficultly comprehending.

The American social psychologist Robert Levine* suggested that "This important book should be required reading not only for social scientists, but also for politicians, decision-makers, educators and just about anyone else disturbed by the self-destructive directions in which the United States and the rest of the world seem to be moving."[8] Levine, like Zimbardo, hopes that knowledge of situational factors will make people less susceptible to their ill effects.

Yet Zimbardo's final message is optimistic and meant as a call to action for general readers: "Each of us may possess the capacity to do terrible things. But we also possess an inner hero; if stirred to action, that inner hero is capable of performing tremendous goodness for others."[9]

1. George R. Mastroianni, "Zimbardo's Apple." *Analyses of Social Issues and Public Policy* 7, no. 1 (2007): 251.

2. Mastroianni, "Zimbardo's Apple," 251.

3. "What is HIP?" Heroic Imagination Project, accessed September 27, 2015, http://heroicimagination. org/.

4. Philip Zimbardo, "What Makes a Hero?" *Greater Good Science Center*, January 18, 2011, accessed September 27, 2015, http://greatergood. berkeley.edu/article/item/what_makes_a_hero.

5. Zeno Franco and Philip Zimbardo, "The Banality of Heroism," *Greater Good Science Center*, September 1, 2006, accessed September 27, 2015, http://greatergood.berkeley.edu/article/item/the_ banality_of_heroism.

6. Franco and Zimbardo, "The Banality of Heroism."

7. Craig Haney, *Reforming Punishment: Psychological Limits to the Pains of Imprisonment.* (Washington DC: American Psychological Association, 2006), x.

8. Robert Levine, "The Evil That Men Do," *American Scientist*, September-October 2007, accessed September 15, 2015, http://www. americanscientist.org/bookshelf/content2/2007/5/the-evil-that-men-do.

9. Zimbardo, "What Makes a Hero?"

GLOSSARY OF TERMS

1. **Abu Ghraib:** a prison in Baghdad where Iraqi prisoners and detainees were held captive during the American-led 2003 invasion of Iraq. A scandal erupted after it was revealed that the prisoners there were subjected to physical, psychological, and sexual abuse by American soldiers.

2. **American Psychological Association (APA):** the scientific and professional organization that represents psychologists in the United States—the largest professional research psychology organization in America.

3. **Amnesty International:** a non-governmental organization originally founded in the 1960s to secure the human rights of political prisoners, now active in the field of human rights more generally.

4. **Association for Psychological Science (APS):** an international nonprofit organization (previously known as the American Psychological Society) concerned with the ethics, interests, and promotion of research in the field of psychology.

5. **Authoritarian:** a personality trait that is associated with both high levels of obedience and submission to authorities, as well as with support for the oppression of subordinates.

6. **Banality of evil:** a phrase that author Hannah Arendt coined to describe the Nazi war criminal Adolf Eichmann, who claimed he'd simply been "doing his job" while overseeing the slaughter of Jews during World War II. The term later came to refer to an idea that evil is commonplace and can be perpetrated by ordinary people.

7. **BBC Prison Study:** an empirical study conducted by social psychologists Stephen Reicher and S. Alexander Haslam and designed as a comparison and contrast to the Stanford Prison Experiment. It was broadcast as a television documentary in 2002 on the British Broadcasting Corporation (BBC).

8. **Behaviorism:** a major theory of learning that dominated psychology throughout the twentieth century, particularly in the middle of the century. Those scholars who supported the theory tended to view cognitive factors (that is, thinking) as less relevant than behaviors and preferred to study observable behaviors.

9. **British Broadcasting Corporation (BBC):** a British television and media broadcaster.

10. **Catholic priest sexual-abuse cases:** a series of allegations and convictions, most commonly in the late twentieth and early twenty-first century, of child sexual abuse committed by members of Catholic Church's clergy.

11. **Cognitions:** all mental abilities and processes associated with knowledge. The term includes memory, attention, problem solving, learning, and others.

12. **Cognitive revolution:** a broad movement beginning in the 1950s in several fields, such as psychology, anthropology, and linguistics. This movement focused on studying the internal thoughts, attitudes, motivations, and values that humans use to make sense of and interact with the world.

13. **Conformity:** a practice whereby individuals match their cognitions and behaviors to that of a group typically due to group norms and other social pressures.

14. **Court-martial:** a military court that typically determines the guilt and sentencing of military members.

15. **Debriefed:** a post-study intervention in research involving human subjects that provides participants with additional information about the study and probes them for psychological strain resulting from it.

16. **Dehumanization:** the act of overlooking or devaluing the human attributes of another person, typically viewing or treating the dehumanized as more impersonal, unequal, or animal.

17. **Deindividuation:** in social psychology, the loss of one's self-awareness and many of one's tendencies due to inclusion in a group or because one is anonymous.

18. **Demand characteristics:** a case where participants in a research study uncover the purpose of the study, which then influences their attitudes or behavior.

19. **Disposition:** in the field of psychology, an individual's internal characteristics, such as personality traits.

20. **Egalitarian:** a social doctrine that advocates treating people equally.

21. **Enron fraud case:** a case that occurred in 2001, when it emerged that Enron Corporation, a giant American energy company, was committing widespread institutionalized corruption and accounting fraud. This scandal resulted in the company's bankruptcy and the jailing of some executives.

22. **Ghetto:** an often poor, segregated section of a city that houses minority groups who generally have few other housing options.

23. **Great Depression:** the most significant economic recession in American history, beginning in 1929 and lasting through much of the 1930s.

24. **Heroic Imagination Project:** a nonprofit organization that Philip Zimbardo founded to research, teach, and promote heroism.

25. **Human Subjects Research Review Board/Institutional review boards (IRBs):** groups that review, monitor, and approve studies involving human participation. They were created in response to the many studies in the early to mid-twentieth century that used undisclosed deception and other means now considered unethical in the treatment of human subjects.

26. **Individualism:** a mindset whereby people think of themselves as individuals more than they think of themselves as members of a group.

27. **Interactionist:** in social and personality psychology, a common view that behavior is largely determined by the interaction of dispositional and situational factors.

28. **Iraq War:** a protracted conflict that began with the American-led invasion of Iraq in 2003.

29. **Lucifer:** in Christian tradition, a fallen angel who became the embodiment of evil.

30. **Mass incarceration:** the imprisonment of people at relatively high rates.

31. **Need to belong:** in psychology, the idea that humans have a fundamental need to feel included and accepted into groups and social circles.

32. **Norms:** in psychology, the accepted standards, values, and expected ways to

behave and think in any given group (from a small group to a wider society or population). Each group defines its own norms, and a norm for one group may be unacceptable for another.

33. **Obedience to authority:** the deference and submission shown to authorities. Work by psychologist Stanley Milgram suggested that obedience to authority has a surprisingly strong influence on many people's behaviors.

34. **Obedience studies:** research that Stanley Milgram conducted at Yale University in the early 1960s in which he instructed volunteers to give electric shocks to a stranger, allegedly for an experiment on learning. Unaware the shocks were not real, most participants administered increasingly powerful shocks, despite their own fear and distress at doing so. This controversial experiment revealed the power that authority figures can have over people's behaviors.

35. **Peer pressure:** the social influence of a group to encourage attitude and behavioral change in peers and other group members.

36. **Personality psychology:** a field of psychology interested in how people differ on meaningful psychological variables.

37. **Person-situation debate:** a controversy found throughout the history of personality psychology concerned with determining the influence of personality/dispositional factors versus situational factors on behavior.

38. **Political scientist:** a person engaged in the systematic study of human political behavior and structures (such as the institutions of government, the ways in which political choices are made, international relations, and so on).

39. **Positive psychology:** a branch of psychology that focuses on the development of achievement rather than the treatment of pathology.

40. **Power of the situation:** the idea that situations have the potential to drastically influence human behavior.

41. **Robber's Cave Experiment:** A 1954 psychology study designed by the social psychologist Muzafer Sherif. He randomly split young boys at a summer camp in Oklahoma into two groups that competed over camp resources, leading to prejudice, negative stereotyping, and group conflict.

42. **Rwanda genocides:** the 1994 mass slaughter of up to one million people in Rwanda. Most victims were from the country's Tutsi ethnic minority group, killed by the Hutu majority.

43. **Sadism/sadistic:** deliberate cruelty or deriving pleasure from abusing others.

44. **Schlesinger report:** an independent investigation into the Abu Ghraib prison-abuse reports led by James Schlesinger in 2004.

45. **Situation:** the aspects of a context that are external to the person, serving as a focal point of analysis to create evil. The situation may mean anything from the surrounding environment, including other people, the weather, external rules and laws, and so on.

46. **Situationists:** people who typically believe that the power of situations significantly determines the behavior of the individuals in those situations, and who generally prefer situational explanations for behavior over those involving personality traits.

47. **Situational forces:** the powerful psychological pressures that the situation around a person places on him or her, whether he or she is aware of those pressures or not.

48. **Sociologist:** someone who studies the history, nature, formation, and structures of human societies.

49. **Social psychology:** a field of psychology interested in how situations influence people's thoughts, emotions, and behaviors.

50. **Solitary confinement:** a form of imprisonment that involves secluding a prisoner in a cell and preventing him or her from having any human contact, even with other prisoners.

51. **Stanford Prison Experiment:** a 1971 psychology study that Philip Zimbardo conducted at Stanford University in which he randomly assigned 12 volunteer participants to the role of either prisoner or guard in a makeshift prison. The experiment, intended to last two weeks, had to be ended early due to the guards' abuse of the prisoners whom they controlled.

52. **Systemic factors:** the influence of large-scale organizations or systems such as

governments, cultures, and economies.

53. **Trait:** in personality psychology, a disposition or somewhat consistent pattern of behavior or cognition.

54. **US Department of Defense (DoD):** a branch of the US government charged with national security and the armed forces.

55. **Vietnam War:** an armed conflict from 1955 to 1975 between North Vietnam and South Vietnam, who were supported by the US military after 1961. All sides, including American troops, committed atrocities.

56. **World War II:** a global conflict that took place from 1939 to 1945 between the Axis Powers (Germany, Italy, and Japan) and the Allies (Great Britain, the Soviet Union, the United States, and other nations).

PEOPLE MENTIONED IN THE TEXT

1. **Solomon Asch (1907–96)** was a Polish social psychologist and professor emeritus at the University of Pennsylvania best known for his work on conformity.

2. **Ali Banuazizi** is an Iranian American political scientist and professor at Boston College known for his work on the political cultures of the Middle East.

3. **Ludy T. Benjamin Jr. (b. 1945)** is an American psychologist and professor at Texas A&M University. His works have documented psychology's transformation into a science.

4. **George W. Bush (b. 1946)** was the 43rd President of the United States. A Republican, he served between 2001 and 2009.

5. **Thomas Carnahan** is an American organizational psychologist and formerly a professor at the University of Memphis. He is known for his work reexamining the Stanford Prison Experiment.

6. **Dick Cheney (b. 1941)** was the 46th Vice President of the United States. A Republican, he served from 2001 to 2009 under President George W. Bush.

7. **Susan T. Fiske (b. 1952)** is an American social psychologist and professor at Princeton University known for her work on social cognition and on prejudice and stereotyping.

8. **Zeno Franco** is an American clinical psychology professor at the Medical College of Wisconsin. His works have researched and defined heroism.

9. **Ivan Frederick (b. 1966)** is a former staff sergeant in the US Army. In 2004, he was convicted of war crimes for his mistreatment of detainees at Abu Ghraib prison in Iraq the previous year. After admitting to multiple charges including conspiracy, maltreatment of detainees, assault and indecent acts, he was sentenced to eight years in prison and dishonorably discharged.

10. **Craig Haney** is an American social psychologist and professor at the University of California at Santa Cruz known for his work on the psychological effects of incarceration and the effectiveness of prisons.

11. **S. Alexander Haslam (b. 1962)** is an Australian social psychologist and professor at the University of Queensland. His works examine conformity and tyranny, and question interpretations of the Stanford Prison Experiment and Stanley Milgram's obedience studies.

12. **Robert Levine** is an American social psychologist and professor at California State University at Fresno known for his work on the use and perception of time by people in different cultures.

13. **George R. Mastroianni** is an American psychologist and professor at the US Air Force Academy. His works apply psychological research to military training and practice.

14. **Rose McDermott** is an American political scientist and professor of international relations at Brown University known for her work on the predictors of political behavior.

15. **Sam McFarland** is an American social psychologist and professor emeritus at Western Kentucky University who focuses on human rights.

16. **Stanley Milgram (1933–84)** was an American social psychologist and professor at Yale University. His famous obedience studies demonstrated the extent to which people will conform to and obey authorities.

17. **Walter Mischel (b. 1930)** is an American psychologist and professor at Columbia University who has studied self-control, and developed an interactionist perspective to personality.

18. **Siamak Movahedi** is an Iranian American sociologist and professor of sociology at the University of Massachusetts. His research includes the study of the relationships between social structure and psychopathology.

19. **Stephen Reicher** is a British social psychologist and professor at the University of St.Andrews. He has studied human behavior in groups and conducted research on leaders and tyranny.

20. **Donald Rumsfeld (b. 1932)** was the 13th United States Secretary of Defense, from 1975 to 1977. He returned to serve as the 21st Secretary of Defense, from 2001 to 2006.

21. **Carolyn Sherif (1922–82)** was an American social psychologist who spent most of her career at Pennsylvania State University. She studied group conflict and cooperation.

22. **Muzafer Sherif (1906–88)** was a Turkish-American social psychologist. His key works were on social norms and the social conflict that results from the competition for resources. He designed the Robber's Cave Experiment.

23. **Joan E. Sieber** is an American psychologist and a professor emerita at California State University known for her work on scientific and research ethics.

24. **Jeffry A. Simpson** is an American social psychologist and professor at the University of Minnesota known for his work examining people's close relationships.

25. **Martin B. Tolich** is a New Zealand sociologist and professor at the University of Otago, New Zealand. His works include studies of research ethics.

WORKS CITED

1. Asch, Solomon E. "Studies of Independence and Conformity: I. A Minority of One Against a Unanimous Majority." *Psychological Monographs: General and Applied* 70, no. 9 (1956): 1–70.

2. Banuazizi, Ali and Siamak Movahedi, "Interpersonal Dynamics in a Simulated Prison: A Methodological Analysis." *American Psychologist* 30, no. 2 (1975): 152–60.

3. Carnahan, Thomas and Sam McFarland. "Revisiting the Stanford Prison Experiment: Could Participant Self-Selection Have Led to the Cruelty?" *Personality and Social Psychology Bulletin* 33, no. 5 (2007): 603–14.

4. Cushman, Jr., John H. "Outside Panel Faults Leaders of Pentagon for Prisoner Abuse." *New York Times*. August 24, 2004. Accessed September 17, 2015, http://www.nytimes.com/2004/08/24/politics/24CND-ABUS.html.

5. Donnellan, M. Brent, et al. "Not So Situational." *Observer*. June/July 2007. Accessed September 27, 2015. http://www.psychologicalscience.org/index.php/publications/observer/2007/june-july-07/not-so-situational.html.

6. Drury, Scott, Scott A. Hutchens, Duane E. Shuttlesworth, and Carole L. White. "Philip G. Zimbardo on His Career and the Stanford Prison Experiment's 40th Anniversary." *History of Psychology* 15, no. 2 (2012): 161–70.

7. Fiske, Susan T., L. T. Harris, and A. J. Cuddy. "Social Psychology. Why Ordinary People Torture Enemy Prisoners." *Science* 306, no. 5701 (2004): 1482–3.

8. Franco, Zeno and Philip Zimbardo, "The Banality of Heroism." *Greater Good Science Center*. September 1, 2006. Accessed September 27, 2015. http://greatergood.berkeley.edu/article/item/the_banality_of_heroism.

9. Haney, Craig. *Reforming Punishment: Psychological Limits to the Pains of Imprisonment*. Washington DC: American Psychological Association, 2006.

10. "A Culture of Harm Taming the Dynamics of Cruelty in Supermax Prisons." *Criminal Justice and Behavior* 35, no. 8 (2008): 956–84.

11. "Counting Casualties in the War on Prisoners." *USFL Rev*. 43 (2008): 87–138.

12. Haney, Craig, Curtis Banks, and Philip Zimbardo, "Interpersonal Dynamics in a Simulated Prison." *International Journal of Criminology and Penology*, 1, (1973): 69–97.

13. Haney, Craig and Philip Zimbardo. "The Past and Future of US Prison Policy: Twenty-five Years after the Stanford Prison Experiment." *American Psychologist* 53, no. 7 (1998): 709–27.

14. Haslam, S. Alexander and Stephen D. Reicher. "Contesting the 'Nature' Of Conformity: What Milgram and Zimbardo's Studies Really Show." *PLoS Biology* 10, no. 11 (2012): e1001426.

15. Herbert, Wray. "The Banality of Evil." *Observer*. April 2007. Accessed September 27, 2015. http://aps.psychologicalscience.org/index.php/publications/observer/2007/april-07/the-banality-of-evil.html.

16. Krakovsky, Marina. "Zimbardo Unbound." *Stanford Magazine*. May/June 2007. Accessed September 27, 2015. https://alumni.stanford.edu/get/page/magazine/article/?article_id=32541.

17. Levine, Robert. "The Evil That Men Do." *American Scientist*. September-October 2007. Accessed September 15, 2015, http://www.americanscientist.org/bookshelf/content2/2007/5/the-evil-that-men-do.

18. Maslach, Christina. "Emperor of the Edge." *Psychology Today*. September 1, 2000. Accessed September 15, 2015, https://www.psychologytoday.com/articles/200009/emperor-the-edge.

19. Mastroianni, George R. "Zimbardo's Apple." *Analyses of Social Issues and Public Policy* 7, no. 1 (2007): 251–254.

20. McDermott, Rose. "Reviewed Work: *The Lucifer Effect: Understanding How Good People Turn Evil* by Philip Zimbardo." *Political Psychology* 28, No. 5 (2007): 644–6.

21. Moorehead-Slaughter, Olivia. "Ethics and National Security." *Monitor on Psychology*. April 2006. Accessed September 17, 2015, http://www.apa.org/monitor/apr06/security.aspx.

22. Mischel, Walter. "Toward a Cognitive Social Learning Reconceptualization of Personality." *Psychological Review* 80, no. 4 (1973): 252–83.

23. Reicher, Stephen and S. Alexander Haslam. "Rethinking the Psychology of Tyranny: The BBC Prison Study." *British Journal of Social Psychology* 45, no. 1 (2006): 1–40.

24. Sieber, Joan E. and Martin B. Tolich. *Planning Ethically Responsible Research*. Thousand Oaks: Sage Publications, 2012.

25. Slavich, George M. "On 50 Years of Giving Psychology Away: An Interview with Philip Zimbardo." *Teaching of Psychology* 36, no. 4 (2009): 278–84.

26. Zimbardo, Philip G. "On the Ethics of Intervention in Human Psychological Research: With Special Reference to the Stanford Prison Experiment." *Cognition* 2, no. 2 (1973): 243–56.

27. "Recollections of a Social Psychologist's Career: An Interview with Dr. Philip Zimbardo." *Journal of Social Behavior and Personality* 14, No. 1 (1999): 1–22.

28. "Power turns good soldiers into 'bad apples.'" *The Boston Globe*. May 9, 2004. Accessed September 16, 2015, http://www.boston.com/news/globe/editorial_opinion/oped/articles/2004/05/09/power_turns_good_soldiers_into_bad_apples/.

29. *The Lucifer Effect: Understanding How Good People Turn Evil.* New York: Random House, 2007.

30. "Person X Situation X System Dynamics." *The Lucifer Effect*. Accessed September 27, 2015. http://www.lucifereffect.com/apsrejoinder.htm.

31. "What Makes a Hero?" *Greater Good Science Center*. January 18, 2011. Accessed September 27, 2015. http://greatergood.berkeley.edu/article/item/what_makes_a_hero/.

32. Zimbardo, Philip G. and John N. Boyd. "Putting Time in Perspective: A Valid, Reliable Individual-Differences Metric." *Journal of Personality and Social Psychology* 77, no. 6 (1999): 1271–88.

33. Zimbardo, Philip G., Christina Maslach, and Craig Haney. "Reflections on the Stanford Prison Experiment: Genesis, Transformations, Consequences." *Obedience to Authority: Current Perspectives on the Milgram Paradigm* (2000): 193–237.

原书作者简介

菲利普·津巴多，生于 1933 年，美国社会心理学家、斯坦福大学荣退教授。他有关邪恶行为诱因的研究使他闻名遐迩，但也引发了不少争议。在 1971 年开展的斯坦福监狱实验中，他发现在模拟监狱中充当狱卒的普通志愿者很快变得恶毒残暴。津巴多后来为一名在伊拉克阿布格莱布监狱中折磨囚犯的美国看守出庭作证。他的著作《路西法效应》于 2007 年出版，他在书中表明，导致这种邪恶行为的往往是"坏木桶"而非"坏苹果"。津巴多撰写了多部心理学研究方面的专著，并获得了许多知名奖项。现如今，津巴多除了积极参与反战、倡导监狱改革外，还继续研究害羞和英雄主义等课题，并激励日常生活中的英雄行为。

本书作者简介

亚历山大·J. 奥康纳博士在加利福尼亚大学伯克利分校完成了博士研究生阶段的学习，获得了社会与人格心理学博士学位。

世界名著中的批判性思维

《世界思想宝库钥匙丛书》致力于深入浅出地阐释全世界著名思想家的观点，不论是谁、在何处都能了解到，从而推进批判性思维发展。

《世界思想宝库钥匙丛书》与世界顶尖大学的一流学者合作，为一系列学科中最有影响的著作推出新的分析文本，介绍其观点和影响。在这一不断扩展的系列中，每种选入的著作都代表了历经时间考验的思想典范。通过为这些著作提供必要背景、揭示原作者的学术渊源以及说明这些著作所产生的影响，本系列图书希望让读者以新视角看待这些划时代的经典之作。读者应学会思考、运用并挑战这些著作中的观点，而不是简单接受它们。

ABOUT THE AUTHOR OF THE ORIGINAL WORK

Born in 1933, **Philip Zimbardo** is an American social psychologist and professor emeritus at Stanford University. His work on triggers of evil behaviour has made him famous yet controversial. In his 1971 Stanford Prison Experiment, he discovered that regular volunteers playing the role of guards in a mock prison quickly became abusive. Zimbardo later testified in defence of a US guard who committed acts of torture in Iraq's Abu Ghraib prison. His 2007 work, *The Lucifer Effect*, suggests it is more often "bad barrels" rather than "bad apples" that lead to such behaviour. Zimbardo has written many books investigating psychology and has received a number of prestigious awards. Now an anti-war and prison-reform activist, he continues to research topics including shyness and heroism, and promotes heroism in everyday life.

ABOUT THE AUTHOR OF THE ANALYSIS

Dr Alexander J. O'Connor did his postgraduate work at the University of California, Berkeley, where he received a PhD for work on social and personality psychology.

ABOUT MACAT
GREAT WORKS FOR CRITICAL THINKING

Macat is focused on making the ideas of the world's great thinkers accessible and comprehensible to everybody, everywhere, in ways that promote the development of enhanced critical thinking skills.

It works with leading academics from the world's top universities to produce new analyses that focus on the ideas and the impact of the most influential works ever written across a wide variety of academic disciplines. Each of the works that sit at the heart of its growing library is an enduring example of great thinking. But by setting them in context — and looking at the influences that shaped their authors, as well as the responses they provoked — Macat encourages readers to look at these classics and game-changers with fresh eyes. Readers learn to think, engage and challenge their ideas, rather than simply accepting them.

批判性思维与《路西法效应》

首要批判性思维技巧：解决问题

次要批判性思维技巧：理性化思维

  是什么让好人也会做坏事，甚至干些罪恶的勾当呢？很少有心理学家能够像菲利普·津巴多那样有资格回答这个问题。他是一位心理学教授，不仅主持开展了堪称经典的斯坦福监狱实验（安排两组学生在一个临时监狱中分别充当囚犯和狱卒，极富戏剧性效果），而且还在第二次海湾战争后积极为一名参与暴力虐待伊拉克战俘的美国军人出庭辩护。

  津巴多撰写的《路西法效应》分析详尽，旨在找到措施以解决"好人也会为恶"这一问题。津巴多运用其解决问题的能力，通过对两种情形的理解找到了问题的答案。他写道，首先，情境因素（环境和背景）肯定比性情因素重要，这意味着即使是一个正派善良的人置身于异常或者有压力的环境之中，他也会一反常态。其次，善和恶并非相互对立，而是可以互相转换。大多数人既可以是天使，也可能成为魔鬼，视环境因素而定。

  在论述过程中，津巴多还以斯坦利·米尔格拉姆的研究为基础，后者曾经开展了一项心理学实验，揭示了权威人士会对下属的行为产生重大影响。同时，津巴多的著作还提出了一些富有建设性的问题，它们超越了理论本身，去思考现实世界中发生的事情，这种重要性不言而喻，也给我们树立了一个很好的榜样。

CRITICAL THINKING AND *THE LUCIFER EFFECT*

• Primary critical thinking skill: PROBLEM-SOLVING
• Secondary critical thinking skill: REASONING

What makes good people capable of committing bad—even evil—acts? Few psychologists are as well-qualified to answer that question as Philip Zimbardo, a psychology professor who was not only the author of the classic Stanford Prison Experiment—which asked two groups of students to assume the roles of prisoners and guards in a makeshift jail, to dramatic effect—but also an active participant in the trial of a US serviceman who took part in the violent abuse of Iraqi prisoners in the wake of the second Gulf War.

Zimbardo's book *The Lucifer Effect* is an extended analysis that aims to find solutions to the problem of how good people can commit evil acts. Zimbardo used his problem-solving skills to locate the solution to this question in an understanding of two conditions. Firstly, he writes, situational factors (circumstances and setting) must override dispositional ones, meaning that decent and well-meaning people can behave uncharacteristically when placed in unusual or stressful environments. Secondly, good and evil are not alternatives; they are interchangeable. Most people are capable of being both angels and devils, depending on the circumstances.

In making this observation, Zimbardo also built on the work of Stanley Milgram, whose own psychological experiments had shown the impact that authority figures can have on determining the actions of their subordinates. Zimbardo's book is a fine example of the importance of asking productive questions that go beyond the theoretical to consider real-world events.

《世界思想宝库钥匙丛书》简介

《世界思想宝库钥匙丛书》致力于为一系列在各领域产生重大影响的人文社科类经典著作提供独特的学术探讨。每一本读物都不仅仅是原经典著作的内容摘要，而是介绍并深入研究原经典著作的学术渊源、主要观点和历史影响。这一丛书的目的是提供一套学习资料，以促进读者掌握批判性思维，从而更全面、深刻地去理解重要思想。

每一本读物分为 3 个部分：学术渊源、学术思想和学术影响，每个部分下有 4 个小节。这些章节旨在从各个方面研究原经典著作及其反响。

由于独特的体例，每一本读物不但易于阅读，而且另有一项优点：所有读物的编排体例相同，读者在进行某个知识层面的调查或研究时可交叉参阅多本该丛书中的相关读物，从而开启跨领域研究的路径。

为了方便阅读，每本读物最后还列出了术语表和人名表（在书中则以星号 * 标记），此外还有参考文献。

《世界思想宝库钥匙丛书》与剑桥大学合作，理清了批判性思维的要点，即如何通过 6 种技能来进行有效思考。其中 3 种技能让我们能够理解问题，另 3 种技能让我们有能力解决问题。这 6 种技能合称为"批判性思维 PACIER 模式"，它们是：

分析：了解如何建立一个观点；
评估：研究一个观点的优点和缺点；
阐释：对意义所产生的问题加以理解；
创造性思维：提出新的见解，发现新的联系；
解决问题：提出切实有效的解决办法；
理性化思维：创建有说服力的观点。

THE MACAT LIBRARY

The Macat Library is a series of unique academic explorations of seminal works in the humanities and social sciences — books and papers that have had a significant and widely recognised impact on their disciplines. It has been created to serve as much more than just a summary of what lies between the covers of a great book. It illuminates and explores the influences on, ideas of, and impact of that book. Our goal is to offer a learning resource that encourages critical thinking and fosters a better, deeper understanding of important ideas.

Each publication is divided into three Sections: Influences, Ideas, and Impact. Each Section has four Modules. These explore every important facet of the work, and the responses to it.

This Section-Module structure makes a Macat Library book easy to use, but it has another important feature. Because each Macat book is written to the same format, it is possible (and encouraged!) to cross-reference multiple Macat books along the same lines of inquiry or research. This allows the reader to open up interesting interdisciplinary pathways.

To further aid your reading, lists of glossary terms and people mentioned are included at the end of this book (these are indicated by an asterisk [*] throughout) — as well as a list of works cited.

Macat has worked with the University of Cambridge to identify the elements of critical thinking and understand the ways in which six different skills combine to enable effective thinking.

Three allow us to fully understand a problem; three more give us the tools to solve it. Together, these six skills make up the PACIER model of critical thinking. They are:

ANALYSIS — understanding how an argument is built
EVALUATION — exploring the strengths and weaknesses of an argument
INTERPRETATION — understanding issues of meaning
CREATIVE THINKING — coming up with new ideas and fresh connections
PROBLEM-SOLVING — producing strong solutions
REASONING — creating strong arguments

"《世界思想宝库钥匙丛书》提供了独一无二的跨学科学习和研究工具。它介绍那些革新了各自学科研究的经典著作,还邀请全世界一流专家和教育机构进行严谨的分析,为每位读者打开世界顶级教育的大门。"

—— 安德烈亚斯·施莱歇尔,
经济合作与发展组织教育与技能司司长

"《世界思想宝库钥匙丛书》直面大学教育的巨大挑战……他们组建了一支精干而活跃的学者队伍,来推出在研究广度上颇具新意的教学材料。"

—— 布罗尔斯教授、勋爵,剑桥大学前校长

"《世界思想宝库钥匙丛书》的愿景令人赞叹。它通过分析和阐释那些曾深刻影响人类思想以及社会、经济发展的经典文本,提供了新的学习方法。它推动批判性思维,这对于任何社会和经济体来说都是至关重要的。这就是未来的学习方法。"

—— 查尔斯·克拉克阁下,英国前教育大臣

"对于那些影响了各自领域的著作,《世界思想宝库钥匙丛书》能让人们立即了解到围绕那些著作展开的评论性言论,这让该系列图书成为在这些领域从事研究的师生们不可或缺的资源。"

—— 威廉·特朗佐教授,加利福尼亚大学圣地亚哥分校

"Macat offers an amazing first-of-its-kind tool for interdisciplinary learning and research. Its focus on works that transformed their disciplines and its rigorous approach, drawing on the world's leading experts and educational institutions, opens up a world-class education to anyone."

—— Andreas Schleicher, Director for Education and Skills, Organisation for Economic Co-operation and Development

"Macat is taking on some of the major challenges in university education... They have drawn together a strong team of active academics who are producing teaching materials that are novel in the breadth of their approach."

—— Prof Lord Broers, former Vice-Chancellor of the University of Cambridge

"The Macat vision is exceptionally exciting. It focuses upon new modes of learning which analyse and explain seminal texts which have profoundly influenced world thinking and so social and economic development. It promotes the kind of critical thinking which is essential for any society and economy. This is the learning of the future."

—— Rt Hon Charles Clarke, former UK Secretary of State for Education

"The Macat analyses provide immediate access to the critical conversation surrounding the books that have shaped their respective discipline, which will make them an invaluable resource to all of those, students and teachers, working in the field."

—— Prof William Tronzo, University of California at San Diego

TITLE	中文书名	类别
An Analysis of Arjun Appadurai's *Modernity at Large: Cultural Dimensions of Globalization*	解析阿尔君·阿帕杜莱《消失的现代性：全球化的文化维度》	人类学
An Analysis of Claude Lévi-Strauss's *Structural Anthropology*	解析克劳德·列维—斯特劳斯《结构人类学》	人类学
An Analysis of Marcel Mauss's *The Gift*	解析马塞尔·莫斯《礼物》	人类学
An Analysis of Jared M. Diamond's *Guns, Germs, and Steel: The Fate of Human Societies*	解析贾雷德·M. 戴蒙德《枪炮、病菌与钢铁：人类社会的命运》	人类学
An Analysis of Clifford Geertz's *The Interpretation of Cultures*	解析克利福德·格尔茨《文化的解释》	人类学
An Analysis of Philippe Ariès's *Centuries of Childhood: A Social History of Family Life*	解析菲力浦·阿利埃斯《儿童的世纪：旧制度下的儿童和家庭生活》	人类学
An Analysis of W. Chan Kim & Renée Mauborgne's *Blue Ocean Strategy*	解析金伟灿 / 勒妮·莫博涅《蓝海战略》	商业
An Analysis of John P. Kotter's *Leading Change*	解析约翰·P. 科特《领导变革》	商业
An Analysis of Michael E. Porter's *Competitive Strategy: Techniques for Analyzing Industries and Competitors*	解析迈克尔·E. 波特《竞争战略：分析产业和竞争对手的技术》	商业
An Analysis of Jean Lave & Etienne Wenger's *Situated Learning: Legitimate Peripheral Participation*	解析琼·莱夫 / 艾蒂纳·温格《情境学习：合法的边缘性参与》	商业
An Analysis of Douglas McGregor's *The Human Side of Enterprise*	解析道格拉斯·麦格雷戈《企业的人性面》	商业
An Analysis of Milton Friedman's *Capitalism and Freedom*	解析米尔顿·弗里德曼《资本主义与自由》	商业
An Analysis of Ludwig von Mises's *The Theory of Money and Credit*	解析路德维希·冯·米塞斯《货币和信用理论》	经济学
An Analysis of Adam Smith's *The Wealth of Nations*	解析亚当·斯密《国富论》	经济学
An Analysis of Thomas Piketty's *Capital in the Twenty-First Century*	解析托马斯·皮凯蒂《21 世纪资本论》	经济学
An Analysis of Nassim Nicholas Taleb's *The Black Swan: The Impact of the Highly Improbable*	解析纳西姆·尼古拉斯·塔勒布《黑天鹅：如何应对不可预知的未来》	经济学
An Analysis of Ha-Joon Chang's *Kicking Away the Ladder*	解析张夏准《富国陷阱：发达国家为何踢开梯子》	经济学
An Analysis of Thomas Robert Malthus's *An Essay on the Principle of Population*	解析托马斯·罗伯特·马尔萨斯《人口论》	经济学

An Analysis of John Maynard Keynes's *The General Theory of Employment, Interest and Money*	解析约翰·梅纳德·凯恩斯《就业、利息和货币通论》	经济学
An Analysis of Milton Friedman's *The Role of Monetary Policy*	解析米尔顿·弗里德曼《货币政策的作用》	经济学
An Analysis of Burton G. Malkiel's *A Random Walk Down Wall Street*	解析伯顿·G.马尔基尔《漫步华尔街》	经济学
An Analysis of Friedrich A. Hayek's *The Road to Serfdom*	解析弗里德里希·A.哈耶克《通往奴役之路》	经济学
An Analysis of Charles P. Kindleberger's *Manias, Panics, and Crashes: A History of Financial Crises*	解析查尔斯·P.金德尔伯格《疯狂、惊恐和崩溃：金融危机史》	经济学
An Analysis of Amartya Sen's *Development as Freedom*	解析阿马蒂亚·森《以自由看待发展》	经济学
An Analysis of Rachel Carson's *Silent Spring*	解析蕾切尔·卡森《寂静的春天》	地理学
An Analysis of Charles Darwin's *On the Origin of Species: by Means of Natural Selection, or The Preservation of Favoured Races in the Struggle for Life*	解析查尔斯·达尔文《物种起源》	地理学
An Analysis of World Commission on Environment and Development's *The Brundtland Report: Our Common Future*	解析世界环境与发展委员会《布伦特兰报告：我们共同的未来》	地理学
An Analysis of James E. Lovelock's *Gaia: A New Look at Life on Earth*	解析詹姆斯·E.拉伍洛克《盖娅：地球生命的新视野》	地理学
An Analysis of Paul Kennedy's *The Rise and Fall of the Great Powers: Economic Change and Military Conflict from 1500–2000*	解析保罗·肯尼迪《大国的兴衰：1500—2000年的经济变革与军事冲突》	历史
An Analysis of Janet L. Abu-Lughod's *Before European Hegemony: The World System A. D. 1250–1350*	解析珍妮特·L.阿布-卢格霍德《欧洲霸权之前：1250—1350年的世界体系》	历史
An Analysis of Alfred W. Crosby's *The Columbian Exchange: Biological and Cultural Consequences of 1492*	解析艾尔弗雷德·W.克罗斯比《哥伦布大交换：1492年以后的生物影响和文化冲击》	历史
An Analysis of Tony Judt's *Postwar: A History of Europe since 1945*	解析托尼·朱特《战后欧洲史》	历史
An Analysis of Richard J. Evans's *In Defence of History*	解析理查德·J.艾文斯《捍卫历史》	历史
An Analysis of Eric Hobsbawm's *The Age of Revolution: Europe 1789–1848*	解析艾瑞克·霍布斯鲍姆《革命的年代：欧洲1789—1848年》	历史

An Analysis of Roland Barthes's *Mythologies*	解析罗兰·巴特《神话学》	文学与批判理论
An Analysis of Simone de Beauvoir's *The Second Sex*	解析西蒙娜·德·波伏娃《第二性》	文学与批判理论
An Analysis of Edward W. Said's *Orientalism*	解析爱德华·W.萨义德《东方主义》	文学与批判理论
An Analysis of Virginia Woolf's *A Room of One's Own*	解析弗吉尼亚·伍尔芙《一间自己的房间》	文学与批判理论
An Analysis of Judith Butler's *Gender Trouble*	解析朱迪斯·巴特勒《性别麻烦》	文学与批判理论
An Analysis of Ferdinand de Saussure's *Course in General Linguistics*	解析费尔迪南·德·索绪尔《普通语言学教程》	文学与批判理论
An Analysis of Susan Sontag's *On Photography*	解析苏珊·桑塔格《论摄影》	文学与批判理论
An Analysis of Walter Benjamin's *The Work of Art in the Age of Mechanical Reproduction*	解析瓦尔特·本雅明《机械复制时代的艺术作品》	文学与批判理论
An Analysis of W. E. B. Du Bois's *The Souls of Black Folk*	解析W.E.B.杜波依斯《黑人的灵魂》	文学与批判理论
An Analysis of Plato's *The Republic*	解析柏拉图《理想国》	哲学
An Analysis of Plato's *Symposium*	解析柏拉图《会饮篇》	哲学
An Analysis of Aristotle's *Metaphysics*	解析亚里士多德《形而上学》	哲学
An Analysis of Aristotle's *Nicomachean Ethics*	解析亚里士多德《尼各马可伦理学》	哲学
An Analysis of Immanuel Kant's *Critique of Pure Reason*	解析伊曼努尔·康德《纯粹理性批判》	哲学
An Analysis of Ludwig Wittgenstein's *Philosophical Investigations*	解析路德维希·维特根斯坦《哲学研究》	哲学
An Analysis of G. W. F. Hegel's *Phenomenology of Spirit*	解析G.W.F.黑格尔《精神现象学》	哲学
An Analysis of Baruch Spinoza's *Ethics*	解析巴鲁赫·斯宾诺莎《伦理学》	哲学
An Analysis of Hannah Arendt's *The Human Condition*	解析汉娜·阿伦特《人的境况》	哲学
An Analysis of G. E. M. Anscombe's *Modern Moral Philosophy*	解析G.E.M.安斯康姆《现代道德哲学》	哲学
An Analysis of David Hume's *An Enquiry Concerning Human Understanding*	解析大卫·休谟《人类理解研究》	哲学

An Analysis of Søren Kierkegaard's *Fear and Trembling*	解析索伦·克尔凯郭尔《恐惧与战栗》	哲学
An Analysis of René Descartes's *Meditations on First Philosophy*	解析勒内·笛卡尔《第一哲学沉思录》	哲学
An Analysis of Friedrich Nietzsche's *On the Genealogy of Morality*	解析弗里德里希·尼采《论道德的谱系》	哲学
An Analysis of Gilbert Ryle's *The Concept of Mind*	解析吉尔伯特·赖尔《心的概念》	哲学
An Analysis of Thomas Kuhn's *The Structure of Scientific Revolutions*	解析托马斯·库恩《科学革命的结构》	哲学
An Analysis of John Stuart Mill's *Utilitarianism*	解析约翰·斯图亚特·穆勒《功利主义》	哲学
An Analysis of Aristotle's *Politics*	解析亚里士多德《政治学》	政治学
An Analysis of Niccolò Machiavelli's *The Prince*	解析尼科洛·马基雅维利《君主论》	政治学
An Analysis of Karl Marx's *Capital*	解析卡尔·马克思《资本论》	政治学
An Analysis of Benedict Anderson's *Imagined Communities*	解析本尼迪克特·安德森《想象的共同体》	政治学
An Analysis of Samuel P. Huntington's *The Clash of Civilizations and the Remaking of World Order*	解析塞缪尔·P.亨廷顿《文明的冲突与世界秩序的重建》	政治学
An Analysis of Alexis de Tocqueville's *Democracy in America*	解析阿列克西·德·托克维尔《论美国的民主》	政治学
An Analysis of John A. Hobson's *Imperialism: A Study*	解析约翰·A.霍布森《帝国主义》	政治学
An Analysis of Thomas Paine's *Common Sense*	解析托马斯·潘恩《常识》	政治学
An Analysis of John Rawls's *A Theory of Justice*	解析约翰·罗尔斯《正义论》	政治学
An Analysis of Francis Fukuyama's *The End of History and the Last Man*	解析弗朗西斯·福山《历史的终结与最后的人》	政治学
An Analysis of John Locke's *Two Treatises of Government*	解析约翰·洛克《政府论》	政治学
An Analysis of Sun Tzu's *The Art of War*	解析孙武《孙子兵法》	政治学
An Analysis of Henry Kissinger's *World Order: Reflections on the Character of Nations and the Course of History*	解析亨利·基辛格《世界秩序》	政治学
An Analysis of Jean-Jacques Rousseau's *The Social Contract*	解析让-雅克·卢梭《社会契约论》	政治学

An Analysis of Odd Arne Westad's *The Global Cold War: Third World Interventions and the Making of Our Times*	解析文安立《全球冷战：美苏对第三世界的干涉与当代世界的形成》	政治学
An Analysis of Sigmund Freud's *The Interpretation of Dreams*	解析西格蒙德·弗洛伊德《梦的解析》	心理学
An Analysis of William James' *The Principles of Psychology*	解析威廉·詹姆斯《心理学原理》	心理学
An Analysis of Philip Zimbardo's *The Lucifer Effect*	解析菲利普·津巴多《路西法效应》	心理学
An Analysis of Leon Festinger's *A Theory of Cognitive Dissonance*	解析利昂·费斯汀格《认知失调论》	心理学
An Analysis of Richard H. Thaler & Cass R. Sunstein's *Nudge: Improving Decisions about Health, Wealth, and Happiness*	解析理查德·H.泰勒／卡斯·R.桑斯坦《助推：如何做出有关健康、财富和幸福的更优决策》	心理学
An Analysis of Gordon Allport's *The Nature of Prejudice*	解析高尔登·奥尔波特《偏见的本质》	心理学
An Analysis of Steven Pinker's *The Better Angels of Our Nature: Why Violence Has Declined*	解析斯蒂芬·平克《人性中的善良天使：暴力为什么会减少》	心理学
An Analysis of Stanley Milgram's *Obedience to Authority*	解析斯坦利·米尔格拉姆《对权威的服从》	心理学
An Analysis of Betty Friedan's *The Feminine Mystique*	解析贝蒂·弗里丹《女性的奥秘》	心理学
An Analysis of David Riesman's *The Lonely Crowd: A Study of the Changing American Character*	解析大卫·理斯曼《孤独的人群：美国人社会性格演变之研究》	社会学
An Analysis of Franz Boas's *Race, Language and Culture*	解析弗朗兹·博厄斯《种族、语言与文化》	社会学
An Analysis of Pierre Bourdieu's *Outline of a Theory of Practice*	解析皮埃尔·布尔迪厄《实践理论大纲》	社会学
An Analysis of Max Weber's *The Protestant Ethic and the Spirit of Capitalism*	解析马克斯·韦伯《新教伦理与资本主义精神》	社会学
An Analysis of Jane Jacobs's *The Death and Life of Great American Cities*	解析简·雅各布斯《美国大城市的死与生》	社会学
An Analysis of C. Wright Mills's *The Sociological Imagination*	解析C.赖特·米尔斯《社会学的想象力》	社会学
An Analysis of Robert E. Lucas Jr.'s *Why Doesn't Capital Flow from Rich to Poor Countries?*	解析小罗伯特·E.卢卡斯《为何资本不从富国流向穷国？》	社会学

An Analysis of Émile Durkheim's *On Suicide*	解析埃米尔·迪尔凯姆《自杀论》	社会学
An Analysis of Eric Hoffer's *The True Believer: Thoughts on the Nature of Mass Movements*	解析埃里克·霍弗《狂热分子：群众运动圣经》	社会学
An Analysis of Jared M. Diamond's *Collapse: How Societies Choose to Fail or Survive*	解析贾雷德·M.戴蒙德《大崩溃：社会如何选择兴亡》	社会学
An Analysis of Michel Foucault's *The History of Sexuality Vol. 1: The Will to Knowledge*	解析米歇尔·福柯《性史（第一卷）：求知意志》	社会学
An Analysis of Michel Foucault's *Discipline and Punish*	解析米歇尔·福柯《规训与惩罚》	社会学
An Analysis of Richard Dawkins's *The Selfish Gene*	解析理查德·道金斯《自私的基因》	社会学
An Analysis of Antonio Gramsci's *Prison Notebooks*	解析安东尼奥·葛兰西《狱中札记》	社会学
An Analysis of Augustine's *Confessions*	解析奥古斯丁《忏悔录》	神学
An Analysis of C. S. Lewis's *The Abolition of Man*	解析 C. S. 路易斯《人之废》	神学

图书在版编目（CIP）数据

解析菲利普·津巴多《路西法效应》：汉、英/亚历山大·J. 奥康纳（Alexander J. O'Connor）著；单文波译.—上海：上海外语教育出版社，2020
（世界思想宝库钥匙丛书）
ISBN 978-7-5446-6510-0

Ⅰ.①解… Ⅱ.①亚… ②单… Ⅲ.①社会心理学-研究-汉、英 Ⅳ.①C912.6

中国版本图书馆CIP数据核字（2020）第145923号

This Chinese-English bilingual edition of *An Analysis of Philip Zimbardo's* The Lucifer Effect Understanding How Good People Turn Evil is published by arrangement with Macat International Limited.
Licensed for sale throughout the world.

本书汉英双语版由Macat国际有限公司授权上海外语教育出版社有限公司出版。
供在全世界范围内发行、销售。

图字：09 - 2018 - 549

出版发行：上海外语教育出版社
　　　　　　（上海外国语大学内）　邮编：200083
电　　话：021-65425300（总机）
电子邮箱：bookinfo@sflep.com.cn
网　　址：http://www.sflep.com
责任编辑：梁瀚杰

印　　刷：上海信老印刷厂
开　　本：890×1240　1/32　印张 6.125　字数 127千字
版　　次：2020 年 11月第 1版　2020 年 11月第 1次印刷
印　　数：2 100 册

书　　号：ISBN 978-7-5446-6510-0
定　　价：30.00 元
本版图书如有印装质量问题，可向本社调换
质量服务热线：4008-213-263　电子邮箱：editorial@sflep.com